CU00970871

David Adam was born in Alnwi
of Danby on the North Yorksl
where he discovered the gift
pattern. His first book of these, *The Edge of Glory*, achieved immediate popularity. He has since published several collections of
prayers and meditations based on the Celtic tradition and the lives
of the Celtic saints. His books have been translated into several
languages, including Finnish and German, and have appeared in
American editions. Many of his prayers have now been set to
music. After thirteen years as Vicar of Holy Island, where he had
taken many retreats and regularly taught school groups on prayer,
David moved to Waren Mill in Northumberland from where he
continues his work and writing.

THE PATH OF LIGHT

Meditations on prayers
from the Celtic tradition

DAVID ADAM

Illustrations by Monica Capoferri

First published in Great Britain in 2009

Society for Promoting Christian Knowledge
36 Causton Street
London SW1P 4ST

British Library Cataloguing-in-Publication Data
A catalogue record for this book is available from the British Library

ISBN 978–0–281–06070–2

1 3 5 7 9 10 8 6 4 2

Typeset by Graphicraft Ltd, Hong Kong
Printed in the UK by CPI Bookmarque, Croydon, CR0 4TD

Produced on paper from sustainable forests

Contents

Introduction

When I was training for the ministry, an elderly member of the Society of the Sacred Mission, who was in part responsible for my training, said, 'What benefit is there if you have talked about God in many lands and yet do not know him?' He went on to explain why the students at Kelham spent much of their time in worship and in silence, for a person needs to know God rather than just about him. I took this to heart then and have tried to live by it most of my life. Only those who make the journey know more than the maps: only those who enjoy the presence of God can truly talk about him.

If we are to know God and not just of him we must build up a relationship with him. Faith is not a set of beliefs but rather a loving relationship with the living God. We have to spend time with him and learn to enjoy his presence. We need to make definite space in our lives or we will allow God to be crowded out by the call and clamour of life. I believe unless we make a fixed time and place to meet with God it is likely we will stop meeting up and fail to be aware of his presence. There is need to talk to God and to be still in his presence. Usually we begin to get to know God when someone else, who knows him, introduces us to him. Sometimes an event in our lives awakens us to his presence. As with any relationship, if it is to continue there is a need to meet up to converse and to share. Take to heart the words of St Paul concerning the risen Lord: 'I want to know Christ and the power of his resurrection' (Philippians 3.10). Get to know him and not just about him. You need a personal relationship with him and not just second-hand information. Your God is not a God relegated to church or history or books for he is with you now.

In my desire to know God, I have found the prayers of others a great help and inspiration. These prayers are not to replace my own words but to help me to formulate what I would like to say. Most prayers that are written down come from people who have spent years getting to know God and for them their prayer is quite personal. Sometimes there is a danger that we just read a prayer, when in fact it was created with passion, or in some difficult situation, and we fail to capture the depth of the prayer. Words alone often fail to convey the relationship of the person who wrote them to their God. There is a danger that much is 'lost in translation'.

For the last forty years I have found inspiration from prayers written by the Celtic peoples of Britain, Ireland and especially from the Hebrides. I have not only used such prayers in teaching about prayer but I have spent time in meditation with them as a guide. I offer you forty such prayers: though I do so with caution as I am aware of an event in the life of Alexander Carmichael that greatly moved him. The writer of the lyric for the song 'Road to the Isles', the Revd Dr Kenneth Macleod, was a close friend and sometimes travelling companion of Alexander Carmichael. In an appreciation of his friend after his death, Dr Macleod told how only Carmichael could acquire the prayers and hymns which were said behind closed doors and when the lights were out. One evening an old man, while carried away with the love of God, allowed Dr Carmichael to take down a singularly beautiful 'going to sleep' prayer. Early the next morning, the old man travelled a round distance of twenty-six miles to exact a pledge that 'his little prayer' should never be allowed to appear in print. 'Think ye that I slept a wink last night for what I had given away? Proud, indeed, shall I be if it gave pleasure to yourself, but I should not like cold eyes to read it in a book.' In Dr Macleod's presence the manuscript was handed back to be burnt there and then – for days and nights after, the music of that prayer haunted the two men. These were songs of the heart and could not be pressed on to paper, for in doing so some of the life would be lost. Much of what I present is my own affair with God, words which have great depth for me and express a personal relationship: I hope that not too much is 'lost in translation'.

It was in a similar mood to the old man of the Isles that the mother of the Ettrick Shepherd, in the Scottish Borders, scolded Sir Walter Scott for having printed some of the songs that she sang for him. 'There was never ane o' my songs prentit till ye prentit them yourself and ye hae spoilt them a'tigether. They were made for singing not for readin' but ye hae broken the charm now and they will never be sung nair mair.'

There is a deep feeling that nothing important can be captured on paper. Caesar said of the Druids that they considered it improper to commit into writing something that was living. This is very much in line with the Tao expression, 'He who speaks does not know, he who knows does not speak.' Again the Orthodox Church has a saying: 'As soon as we start speaking of the mysteries of God, we hear the gates of heaven closing.' Yet we seek to communicate that which is beyond words and to share with each other the presence and power of God which is beyond description. Come and share with me the mystery and wonder of the presence and love of God.

The God Who Is

AFFIRMING THE PRESENCE

> I believe, O God of all gods,
> That thou art the eternal Father of life;
> I believe, O God of all gods,
> That Thou art the eternal Father of love.
>
> I believe, O God of all gods,
> That thou art the eternal Father of the saints;
> I believe, O God of all gods,
> That Thou art the eternal Father of each one.
>
> I believe, O God of all gods,
> That thou art the eternal Father of mankind;
> I believe, O God of all gods,
> That Thou art the eternal Father of the world.
>
> I believe, O Lord and God of all the peoples,
> That Thou art the creator of the high heavens,
> That Thou art the creator of the skies above,
> That Thou art the creator of the oceans below.
> (*Carmina Gadelica* III, p. 41)

This prayer has the title of 'Morning Prayer' and it was said as a way to begin the day in communication with God.

How do you welcome the day? Do you feel the need to switch on the radio or television? Do you drift into day without thought and with your eyes still half closed or do you welcome it with a joyful affirmation? It is important to give a period of attentiveness to the beginning of each day. We need to rouse ourselves out of ourselves and to an awareness of all that is around us. The cellist Pablo Casals, when he was ninety-three, wrote of how he had welcomed the day for the past eighty years:

1

I go to the piano and I play two preludes and fugues of Bach . . .
It is a sort of benediction on the house. But that is not its only
meaning . . . It is a rediscovery of the world in which I have the
joy of being a part. It fills me with awareness of the wonder of life,
with a feeling of the incredible marvel of being human.

(Quoted in *Song of the Birds*, compiled by
Julian Lloyd Webber, Robson Books, 1985)

At the beginning of the twentieth century Mary Gillies, a crofter
of Morar, welcomed the day by affirming her belief in the God,
the eternal Father of life and love who is ever present, by singing
her morning prayer. What a wonderful start to the day it is. Here
is where all meditation should begin, affirming the presence,
acknowledging:

God is: God is present: God is here: God is with us now.
God is our Father: God gives us life: God gives us love.
    God is the living God.
God is Father not only to the saints but to each one of us,
    of you.
God is the creator of all peoples and of all that there is.
It is God who gives us that mystery we call life.

Affirm this reality. Take time to do it: tune in to the ever present
God who is with you always. Affirmation is not making a request,
it is seeking to be open to the reality of the world and of God. It is
not just positive thinking, it is far more than this, for it is not seeking to make something happen but rather to open your eyes, your
heart and mind to the reality of what is. The Lord is here!

Here are some words to inspire from Teilhard de Chardin:

God, in all that is most living and incarnate in him, is not far away
from us, altogether apart from the world we see, touch hear, smell,
and taste about us. Rather he awaits us every instant, in our action,
in the work of the moment. There is a sense in which he is at the
tip of my pen, my spade, my brush, my needle – of my heart and
my thought.

(Pierre Teilhard de Chardin, *Le Milieu Divin*,
Fontana Books, 1964, p. 64)

On a simple level, I have used this prayer with children as a 'pointing game'. A child says, 'I believe, O God that you are', and points to another child. Then we all give two claps with our hands to give that child time to think. The second child then replies, 'The eternal Father of . . .' and then has to add a word to show what God is the Father of. Words like 'the world', 'the stars', 'the universe', 'love', 'light', 'Jesus', 'my mum', 'my dog', all often appear. As with pointing games, if a word has been used it has not to be used again in this round. When the session is to be brought to an end the leader gives an extra two claps and says, 'God, you are here and with us now.' Adult groups have used this as a quiet time of affirmation and meditation.

Another way to affirm the presence of God and your love for him is to take just a few words and then slowly decrease the words as you seek to enter into a relationship with God:

> I believe, O God of all gods, that you are the eternal Father of life.
> O God of all gods, that you are the eternal Father of life;
> O God of all gods you are
> O God of all gods,
> O God.

When a prayer is used in this way words begin to vibrate with depth and meaning. It is a means of approaching the presence and then resting in God. After a while the words 'O God' carry with them the rest of the prayer and act as an entrance to the heart of God.

Think upon the depth of these words from the poet Kabir found on a fountain in India:

> I laugh when I hear that the fish in the sea are thirsty:
> I laugh when I hear man goes in search of God.

THE STOWE MISSAL

Father, all-powerful and ever-loving
We do well always and everywhere to give you thanks
Through Jesus Christ our Lord.
You O Father with your only begotten Son and the
    Holy Spirit are God.
You are God, one holy and immortal
You are God, incorruptible and unmoving
You are God, invisible and yet ever present
You are God, wonderful and worthy of all praise.
You are God, most high and magnificent
You are God, wise and all powerful
You are God, holy and splendid
You are God, awesome and peace loving
You are God, beautiful and righteous
You are God, blessed and just
You are God, tender and most holy.

You are God, not in singularity of one person
but in the Trinity of one substance
We believe in you;
We bless you
We adore you; and we praise your name for evermore.
We praise you through Jesus Christ who is the salvation of
    the Universe.
Through Christ who is the life of all human beings
Through Christ who is the resurrection of the dead.
Through him the angels and archangels praise your majesty.
With them we praise your great and glorious name
Forever praising you and saying . . .

(eighth to tenth century)

The Stowe Missal gets its name from being in the Stowe library of the Dukes of Buckingham from the nineteenth century. The missal is sometimes called the Lorrha Missal as it was used in the monastery of St Ruadhan in Lorrha, County Tipperary, Ireland. The missal is written in two different hands: one from the mid-eighth century, the second from the tenth century. The actual Mass in the missal may be as early as the sixth century and is the fullest example we have of the Divine Liturgy from the rites of the Celtic branch of the Church. The above Preface prayer, which precedes the saying of the Sanctus, is of Irish origin and not known in any other rite. This missal is small enough for a priest to carry around on his travels and his visiting of Christian communities. The missal is now in the Royal Irish Academy.

I have chosen this Preface because it affirms the presence of God like the first prayer in this book. Our daily prayer should enrich our Sunday worship and our Sunday worship need be reflected in our daily life or it becomes meaningless.

The Preface from the Communion Prayer of consecration does not face the congregation and supply them with directions or information on the church seasons: it faces towards the ever present God in worship, reaching out towards him in deep adoration and love. Word after word has such depth of meaning we could lose ourselves in their fullness and we are invited to lose ourselves in the fullness and love of God.

There are times when the priest turns to the congregation to teach and to inform; here he turns to God in love and adoration: such an action is worth more than a wealth of words. The main work of a priest can be seen and experienced here: it is not so much to teach as to draw people to God through the love that God has for us.

'You are God': we are not dealing with a historic reminder but we are entering into a deeper communion with the ever present God by opening our lives to him. We reach out beyond our small area of knowledge, our small vision to that which only the heart can grasp. The writer of *The Cloud of Unknowing* says, 'Although we cannot have knowledge of God, we can love him: by love he may be touched and embraced, by thought never.' And John Chrysostom says, 'Find the door of your heart, you will discover it is the door to the kingdom of God.'

As the Celtic worshipper was in daily communion with God, to go to the Eucharist was to share in that same communion. You cannot go to communion when you are already part of it. There is only one communion; it is the oneness of the universe, the one Word of God. We are in a world where everything is connected;

we are all 'hitched' to each other: and we are one in the Lord. We have a common union with the earth and a common union with God, a common union with the saints and with the angels of heaven. In that one communion earth and heaven are one. This is expressed simply by a prayer from the Hebrides: 'I find Thee throned in my heart, my Lord Jesus. It is enough. I know that Thou art throned in heaven. My heart and heaven are one.'

God is, is present with us and 'with angels and archangels and all the company of heaven'. In him we are all one. Rejoice in this fellowship and that we dwell in him and he in us. You may like to spend some time with these words about our common union with God and each other, for they present us with a way of looking at life:

> All the communions of a life-time are one communion.
> All communions of all men now living are one communion.
> All communions of all men, present, past and future are one communion.
>
> (Teilhard de Chardin, *Le Milieu Divin*, p. 124)

COME I THIS DAY

> Come I this day to the Father,
> Come I this day to the Son,
> Come I this day to the Holy Spirit powerful:
> I come this day with God,
> I come this day with Christ,
> I come this day with the Spirit of kindly balm.
>
> God, and Spirit, and Jesus,
> From the crown of my head
> To the soles of my feet;
> Come I with my reputation,

Come I with my testimony,
Come I to Thee, Jesu –
Jesu, shelter me.

(Carmina Gadelica I, p. 69)

Many of the Celtic prayers are from an oral tradition and a lay
spirituality of hearth, home and heart. They have been handed
down in families and in communities for generations. Such
prayers are not associated with one day of the week or with going
to church. They are the Church praying in their home environ-
ment, at work and in their travels. Daily they 'come to' and
acknowledge that God 'comes to us'.

There is a sense in which God waits upon us. God does not
force himself upon us but in love waits for us to turn to him. One
of the finest illustrations of this is the story of the Prodigal Son
who went off into a far country. Once this son decided to turn
around and to come to his father he found that his father ran
towards him to enfold him in his loving arms (Luke 15.20). We
should learn from the story of the Prodigal Son that Christianity
is not so much about judgement as about the embracing love of
God and being embraced by God, which is our redemption. In our
coming to God we come to the God of love. He is waiting at this
moment for us to turn to him. He waits upon you.

There is need each day to affirm our turning to God, our coming to him. It is not that God has been absent but rather that we
have ignored or become unaware of the eternal presence. We have
dislocated ourselves, that is we have placed ourselves in hell! For
hell is where God is not present. God has not placed us there, it
is our choice. Let us turn back to God. When the Prodigal Son
decided he had taken the wrong course he made the decision,
'I will arise and go to my father' (Luke 15.18, AV). There is a sense
in which every turning to God, the God of life, is a resurrection:
Come at this very moment and enter the stillness of trust: wait
upon God for he waits for you.

Sit as comfortably as you can. Let go of all tension, check over
your body starting with your head, neck and shoulders. Relax, ease
any points of tension. Make sure all is at ease, for if not you will
soon be distracted.

Know that you are in the presence. Affirm it; say, 'The Lord is here'.

Be aware that God seeks to enfold you in his love.

Still your body and your mind and wait in eager attention, open to him who comes.

Know that you are in his presence, love and care.

If your mind wanders, you may like a few words to still your mind, such as 'Abba, Father', 'Jesus my Lord', 'Spirit of God', '*Maranatha*, come Lord'. As you breathe in, say your chosen word in your heart, but the more stillness and alertness waiting upon God you can achieve the better.

Affirming the presence does not bring God to us, though there is a sense of 'draw near to God and he will draw near to you'. God is always there, it is we who are often only half there at the best with our divided attention and wandering thoughts. There is a great need for us all to make a conscious period of attentiveness to God each day. We should not let anything distract us from doing this. For this reason it is necessary to have a fixed time and a fixed meeting place. Too often those without a fixed time and place fail to meet up. We should not come to God as if we are in a hurry to move on to something else. We need to learn to enjoy the presence of God and to relax in his presence. The prayer for today talks of the 'balm' and the 'peace' of God; these are gifts of the presence. Learn to rest in God and allow God to refresh, heal and restore you. Such abiding in the presence gives us strength and hope for the day.

Why are we so unwilling to give our time to prayer? We do not organize our day to include moments of stillness and peace when we can be in contact with the very source of our being. Why do we talk so much and are so unwilling to listen? We are always occupied and have no room left for prayer. We spend our time in noise and bustle and rarely take time out to talk to our God. We seem to be afraid to be alone or to have a time that might be empty and yet we need this to get to know our God. Without this we cannot grow in the faith, for faith is a living personal relationship with God, not ideas about him. In one single session of stillness and coming to God we can get more refreshment than we would from many books or conversations. It is when we open to him that he can pour his being into us. Remember he will not force himself upon us. It is in him we are renewed and discover the power of his resurrection. It is through our nearness to him and our relationship with him that we become filled with his Spirit and then a blessing to others.

At every moment God seeks entry into your heart. He gives you the opportunity to be part of his kingdom. You are offered the opportunity to live in the kingdom of light, the very kingdom of God, or to go your own way and walk on still in the darkness. Why do you not choose? Why not leave the darkness and walk in hope? Leave your loneliness and learn to walk with God.

Here are some words from a book that first helped me to be aware of the presence of God:

> Remember, I pray you, what I have often recommended to you, which is, to often think on God, by day, by night, in your business and even in your diversions. He is always near you and with you: leave Him not alone. You would think it rude to leave a friend alone, who had come to visit you: why then must God be neglected? Do not then forget Him, think often of Him, adore Him unceasingly, live and die with Him: this is the glorious employment of a Christian, in a word this is our profession; if we do not know it we must learn it.
>
> (Brother Lawrence, *The Practice of the Presence of God*,
> H. R. Allenson, 1906, p. 51)

THE PATH OF RIGHT

When the people of the Isles come out in the morning to their tillage, to their fishing, to their farming, or any of their various occupations anywhere, they say a short prayer called 'Ceum na Corach', 'The Path of Right', 'The Just or True Way'. If the people feel secure from being overseen or overheard, they croon, or sing or intone their morning prayer in a pleasing musical manner. If, however, any person, and especially if a stranger, is seen in the way, the people hum the prayer in an inaudible undertone peculiar to themselves, like the soft murmur of the everlasting murmuring sea, or like the far-distant eerie sighing of the wind among trees, or like the muffled cadence of far-away waters, rising and falling upon the fitful autumn wind.

> My walk this day with God,
> My walk this day with Christ,
> My walk this day with Spirit,
> The Threefold all kindly:
> Ho! ho! ho! the Threefold all kindly.
>
> My shielding this day from ill,
> My shielding this night from harm,
> Ho! Ho! both my soul and my body,
> Be by Father, by Son, by Holy Spirit.
>
> Be the Father shielding me,
> Be the Son shielding me,
> Be the Spirit shielding me,
> As Three and as One:
> Ho! ho! ho! as Three and as One.
> (*Carmina Gadelica* III, p. 49)

There is need to remind ourselves of the presence of God throughout the day. Our prayers should not be restricted to a single period or one place but should be strengthened by turning to God often during our daily activities. Arrow prayers, little darts of love directed at God, are a wonderful way of keeping in contact with God who is with us.

Note how the people of the Isles said this prayer as they came to their work place, to farm, to boat or anywhere. In fact they sang their prayer. I like the idea that they actually would hum their prayer. They were so used to the prayer vibrating in their lives that to hum it brought them the same awareness of their walking and working with God. It is only by letting certain ideas resound day by day that they become part of our whole being. The Church of the Isles knew the value of 'recital theology', of using words and prayers over and over until they resonated in the depths of their being. There is a great need to learn prayers by heart that is in worship rather than by rote. Prayers are more about our heart being in tune with God than with learning words.

Too often we give the impression that prayers are something attached to the Church and not to our day-to-day life. We are in the danger of giving the impression that God is more concerned about the Church than he is about the world which he loves. God is concerned with, is present in, all of life. He is there when we travel to work, in the office, in the shop, when we are oppressed or frustrated, and in our joys and celebrations. Even when we forget or ignore him he is still with us.

There is a great need for Christians to show that they enjoy the presence of God in the world. Faith and prayer are not rules laid down but are rather an entering into an exciting relationship with the Creator, Redeemer and Strengthener, with the God who is with us at all times.

Our lives need to reveal our joy in spending time with God: that we love being in God's presence. We would put ourselves out to spend time with a loved one. If we truly love God, we will gladly do the same. If we do not make room for God in our daily lives, it tells us we are not all that attached to him. Fortunately, God still loves us and is with us. He offers himself to us but we turn away to other things. True, he works with us, but if we ignore him, we fail to grow in love and in the joy of his presence. Without a truly loving relationship with God, our faith cannot grow. God becomes a theory to be discussed rather than a presence to be enjoyed. Only after we have spent time with God and learned of his love for us can we convey that love to others. It is little use speaking of the love of God or of his presence if we do not personally enjoy these realities day by day. It is through our nearness to him and our relationship with him that we become filled with his being and a blessing to others.

At every moment God seeks entry into your heart. He gives you the opportunity to be part of his kingdom. You are offered the opportunity to live in the kingdom of light, the very kingdom of God, or to go your own way and walk on still in the darkness. Why do you not choose? Why not leave the darkness and walk in hope? Leave your loneliness and learn to walk with God. Here is a challenge for you to take up from Brother Lawrence:

> One way to recall easily the mind in the time of prayer, and preserve it more in rest, is not to let it wander too far at other times. You should keep it strictly in the Presence of God, and being accustomed to think of him often from time to time, you will find it easy to keep your mind calm at the time of prayer, or at least recall it from its wanderings.
>
> (Brother Lawrence, *The Practice of the Presence of God*, p. 47)

Now take to heart these words:

> The one who is present everywhere and fills everything is coming. He is coming to fulfil among you the salvation offered to all. Welcome him who welcomed everything that pertains to our human nature. (St Andrew of Crete, *c.* 660–740)

GOD OF ALL

> Our God is the God of all,
> The God of heaven and earth,
> Of the sea and of the rivers;
> The God of the sun and of the moon and of all the stars;
> The God of the God of the lofty mountains
> and of the lowly valleys
> He has His dwelling around heaven and earth,
> and sea, and all that in them is.
> He inspires all,
> He gives life to all,
> He dominates all,
> He supports all.
> He lights the light of the sun.
> He furnishes the light of the night.
> He has made springs in dry land . . .

He is the God of heaven and earth,
of sea and rivers,
of sun moon and stars,
of the lofty mountain and the lowly valley,
the God above heaven,
and in heaven,
and under heaven.

(St Patrick, *c.* 385–461)

Because the modern world is so full of images and offers an abundance of experience we are in danger of losing a sense of appreciation, of wonder and awe. It is too easy to take the world around us for granted. We move from one thing to another and fill our lives with sound, leaving little room for stillness or entering into the depths of the reality that is all about us. We need to become more focused and aware of the mystery of life, the sacredness of all creation. We need be aware of what lives truly depend upon and to have a deep respect towards it.

It is often only by giving our full attention to the world around us that our eyes and our heart are opened. If we are not good at giving our attention to the world and to others it is not likely we will give our attention to God. I often take to heart the words of Jesus to his disciples: 'Are your hearts hardened? Do you have eyes, and fail to see? Do you have ears, and fail to hear? (Mark 8.17–18). If we do not focus on the world properly we will go through life in a blur. If we do not appreciate the deep mystery of being it is unlikely we will come before the loving mystery of God. This mystery is often described as the 'glory of God' and is about a hidden presence that is ever near.

The world is full of the glory of God; his hidden presence is everywhere waiting to be found. You should at least have some of the experience expressed by William Wordsworth even if you could not put it in such words:

And I have felt
A presence that disturbs me with the joy
Of elevated thoughts; a sense sublime
Of something far more deeply interfused,
Whose dwelling is the light of setting suns,

13

And the round ocean and the living air,
And the blue sky, and in the mind of man.
('Tintern Abbey', lines 93–100)

The world in which we live is waiting to reveal God to us. Yet, it is a world we treat with disrespect and boredom; we fail to see that every place is holy, all is able to reveal the presence. It always makes me sad when Christians seem to suggest we should not love the world. This is the world God gives us and he communicates to us through it. The world is not only his creation but he loves it. He wants us to look at it with eyes of love and to care for it. We need to see that God 'gives life to all, he inspires all'.

This is beyond our intellect but it is not beyond our experience. The way to a deeper seeing and hearing is to keep ourselves attentive, alert to what is about us. To be there in a self-forgetfulness that learns to concentrate on what is before us. This will often demand from us stillness and an openness which only comes with practice, though this is not as hard as it seems. I have often experienced this in bird watching. Watching and waiting with every sense alert, knowing the bird is near and will come: or at least putting ourselves in a position where it is possible for this encounter to happen. Here are two thoughts to ponder:

Who surveying the whole scheme of things, is so childish as not to believe that there is a divinity in everything, clothed in it, embracing it, residing in it? For everything that is depends on Him-who-is.
(Gregory of Nyssa, Catechetical Oration 25)

We have only had to go a little beyond the frontier of sensible appearances in order to see the divine welling up and showing through. But it is not only close to us, in front of us, that the divine presence has revealed itself. It has sprung up so universally, and we find ourselves so surrounded and transfixed by it, that there is no room left to fall down and adore it, even within ourselves. By means of all created things, without exception, the divine assails us, penetrates us and moulds us. We imagine it as distant and inaccessible, whereas in fact live steeped, in its burning layers. In eo vivimus.
(Teilhard de Chardin, *Le Milieu Divin*,
Collins Fontana, 1975, p. 112)

The Trinity

BAPTISM BY THE KNEE-WOMAN

When a child comes into the world, the knee-woman puts three drops of water on the forehead of the poor little infant, who has come home to us from the bosom of the everlasting Father. And the woman does this in the name and in the reverence of the kind and powerful Trinity, and says thus:

> In the name of God
> In the name of Jesus
> In the name of the Spirit
> The perfect Three of power
>
> The little drop of the Father
> On thy little forehead, beloved one.
>
> The little drop of the Son
> On thy little forehead, beloved one.
>
> The little drop of the Spirit
> On thy little forehead, beloved one.
>
> To aid thee, to guard thee,
> To shield thee, to surround thee . . .
>
> A little drop of the three
> To shield thee from the sorrow.
>
> A little drop of the three
> To fill thee with Their pleasantness.
> A little drop of the three
> To fill thee with Their virtue.
> (*Carmina Gadelica* III, pp. 17–19)

In the Hebrides the affirmation that we come from God and are immersed in his presence is made at the birth of each child. As soon as it is born the child is acknowledged to be in the 'love and friendliness of God'. Where a priest may not be available for some time due to storms at sea or deep snow and where infant mortality was often high, it was considered important to see that the child was baptized. This baptism was done in the home with neighbouring women in attendance and was done by the knee-woman, which is the one who saw the child into the world. This was known as the 'birth baptism' or the 'knee-woman baptism'. One such woman said, 'When the image of God is born into the world I put three drops of water on the child's forehead. I put the first little drop in the name of the Father, and the watching-women say Amen. I put the second little drop in the name of the Son, and the watching-women say Amen. I put the third little drop in the name of the Spirit, and the watching-women say Amen. And I beseech the Holy Three to lave and to bathe the child and to preserve it to Themselves. And the watching-women say Amen. All the people in the house are raising their voices with the watching-women, giving witness that the child has been committed to the Trinity.'

Later the child will be received formally into the Church by the whole local community and be baptized (again!) by the priest or minister. This baptism was called the 'great baptism', the 'priest baptism' or the 'Church baptism.' This was usually followed by the baptismal feast, a social occasion where the child was handed from one person to another in turn and each would call down a blessing upon the child. If a child had not received one of these baptisms, lay or clerical, the father was held responsible and was considered neglectful in his duty by the local community.

Here we get a glimpse of a group of ordinary people fulfilling our Lord's command, 'Go therefore make disciples of all nations, baptizing them in the name of the Father and of the Son and of the Holy Spirit.' The child is immersed in the ever present Presence. It is a great loss when we concentrate on water baptism when Christ's command was to baptize, to immerse, in 'the name', in the very being of God, Father, Son and Holy Spirit. We are called to rejoice daily, immerse ourselves daily, in the love of the Threefold God, to acknowledge the presence of the Creator, the Redeemer and the indwelling Spirit. To do this does not make God come to us, for God is ever present, but it does makes us more aware of the reality and therefore more able to live in this awareness.

Many a service begins with this immersion, with making ourselves aware that 'we dwell in him', as when we start with the words, 'In the name of the Father, the Son and the Holy Spirit'. Sometimes to this is added the signing of the cross, a greater reminder of our baptism, of our immersion in God and that we were signed with the cross. Sometimes the service will begin with a phrase such as, 'The Lord be with you' or 'The Lord is here': these are not requests but a statement of a reality and it is a pity if we miss the depth of these words. I would some time like to say to a congregation, 'The Lord is here' and then say no more. What more could you want!

Wherever you are, whatever is happening to you, the Lord is with you. Do not rush beyond this point, stop and acknowledge that you are immersed in the grace and goodness of God, Father, Son and Holy Spirit. Affirm the reality you are at this very moment in the love and light of the Lord, Father, Son and Holy Spirit.

It is good to affirm the presence throughout the day. The prayers which follow in this section show how the Celtic peoples made it their business to give their attention to the threefold God at various points in the day and in all their different activities. Throughout their lives from birth to death it was a regular practice to remind themselves they are in the presence of the Holy Three. This began with rising and washing, reviving the fire in the hearth, and continued through the working day and ended with the 'smooring' of the fire and prayers for sleeping.

Remind yourself that you are immersed in God. Affirm your baptism every day. You might like to make the sign of the cross and say simply, 'In the name of the Father and of the Son and of the Holy Spirit.'

Think on these words of Julian of Norwich and make them your own:

> The Trinity is God, and God is the Trinity.
> The Trinity is our maker and keeper.

The Trinity is our everlasting lover, our joy and our bliss,
through our Lord Jesus Christ.
(Julian of Norwich, *Enfolded in Love*, Darton,
Longman and Todd, 1980, p. 1)

ST PATRICK'S BREASTPLATE

I bind unto myself today
the strong name of the Trinity,
by invocation of the same,
the Three in One and One in Three.
(attributed to St Patrick,
tr. Mrs C. F. Alexander)

It is not difficult to imagine St Patrick, on arising, saying this prayer as he put on his tunic and bound it around himself. As he pulled on the lacing he would say, 'I bind unto myself', and acknowledge he was not only wrapped and protected by his clothes but more so by the Three in One and One in Three. This prayer is often known as 'St Patrick's Breastplate'. Just as he would fasten a piece of armour around him to protect his well-being so he puts on the 'armour of the presence of God'. In doing this Patrick is acting out the reality of his baptism, the truth that he is surrounded by and immersed in the presence of God.

It is easy to romanticize the life of Patrick yet it was full of hardship and danger. When he was hardly sixteen, he was captured and taken away from his homeland in Britain to be a slave in Ireland. He was made to look after cattle out in the woods and on the mountainsides through snow, frost and rain. It was at this time he learnt to turn to God in prayer. He tells of how he prayed about a hundred times during the day and in the night nearly the same. Here in captivity he rejoiced in and immersed himself in the presence of the Trinity.

Patrick escaped from this captivity, but after being able to spend some time back at home he felt the call to take the gospel to the land from which he escaped. He tells of suffering greatly, of being reproached, of being persecuted and even of being in chains. He says how he is willing to die for Christ. He has no fear of death for he believes in the love of the holy Three and in the resurrection through Jesus Christ. His faith did not save him from many troubles but it gave him the courage to venture. Patrick knows he is not left alone. He is in the presence of God and that gives him the courage to be.

We need to learn to bind to ourselves the strong Name of the Trinity. Each day we should call upon our God. It is not that God has gone away, for he is always with us. It is our lives that are in danger of being out of tune. In some ways prayer is like tuning a radio or a television. The sound waves are all around but we do not hear them unless we tune in. We do not make the sound waves come; they are already there and are even flowing through us. We tune in and then receive the benefits. There is a sense in which we cannot ask God to come to us for he is already with us. We are surrounded and immersed in his presence. There is need to tune in to that reality. Stop now and rejoice that the Lord is here!

When we say, 'In the name of the Father and of the Son and of the Holy Spirit', we are affirming the presence. 'In the name' is shorthand for all that God is, so I like to sometimes extend this and say, 'In the presence, in the power and in the peace of God, Father, Son and Holy Spirit'. Then leave some time to rejoice in this reality.

You may like to begin, 'In the grace, goodness and guiding of God . . .' or 'In the light, in the love, in the leading of God . . .' Above all it is important to be still and rest in the reality of his presence. Remember no words can make God come: God is here with you. A former bishop of Newcastle did not like saying 'The Lord is here' in church because for many it implied that this is where God is kept. He wanted the words used more in workplaces, in homes, in hospitals and in prisons, in fact wherever people found themselves. In the same way he wanted the words to be used by people, and not priests alone, in their arriving in any new place or situation.

The prayer of binding oneself to the presence of the Holy Three should act like throwing a stone in a pond: the results should ripple out to include all people and all of life. It is good to quietly 'bind' others in the power and peace of God. I tell godparents that it is their duty and their joy to immerse their godchild every day in the presence. If they do this for their godchild it will make a difference not only to their godchild but also to their own lives as they are tuning in to the presence of God.

Patrick's love for God is expressed in a Trinitarian formula, but in fact it is his experience of the Sacred Three that makes him speak this way: it is the person who lives the life that understands the theology of the Trinity. Patrick was in no doubt that

> The Father created us out of His love and for His love.
> The Son redeemed us by His love and for His love.
> The Spirit sustains us with His love and for His love.
> The Holy Three seek us in love and for love.

Patrick says in the Confession:

> In measure, therefore, of the faith of the Trinity it behoves me to distinguish without shrinking from danger, to make known the gift of God, and His everlasting consolation and without fear to spread faithfully everywhere the name of God, in order that even after my death I may leave it as a bequest to my brethren, and to my sons, whom I have baptised in the Lord – so many thousand men.
>
> (Charles H. H. Wright, *The Writings of St Patrick*,
> Religious Tract Society, p. 52)

RUNE BEFORE PRAYER

Old people in the Isles sing this or some other short hymn before prayer. Sometimes the hymn and prayer are intoned in low, tremulous unmeasured cadences like the moving and moaning, the soughing and sighing, of the ever-murmuring sea on their own wild shores. They generally retire to a closet, to an outhouse, to the lee of a knoll, or to the shelter of a dell, that they may not be seen or heard of men. I have known men and women of eighty, ninety, and a hundred years of age continue the practice of their lives in going from one to two miles to the seashore to join their voices with the voicing of the waves, and their praises with the praises of the ceaseless sea.

> I am bending my knee
> In the eye of the Father who created me,
> In the eye of the Son who purchased me,
> In the eye of the Spirit who cleansed me,
> In friendship and affection.
> Through Thine own Anointed One, O God,
> Bestow upon us fullness in our need,
> Love towards God,
> The affection of God,
> The smile of God,
> The wisdom of God,
> The grace of God,
> The fear of God,
> And the will of God
> To do on the world of the Three,
> As angels and saints
> Do in heaven;
> Each shade and light,
> Each day and night,
> Each time in kindness,
> Give Thou us Thy Spirit.
> (*Carmina Gadelica* I, pp. 2–3)

For our faith to deepen it is necessary to withdraw from the business of the day and the busyness of the day. We need to make space in our lives for God to enter. Too often when God comes to us he experiences what St Joseph did when he came to the inn that said 'no room'. We put off our prayers, our time with God, because we are too busy; we are already occupied and when God seeks us out he finds us pre-occupied. If we do not make that space and time of stillness, there is a danger that we are always preoccupied and when people seek to communicate with us they have the same problem that God encounters. We are not quite present. There is a great danger that preoccupation does not let us live in the now. We are unaware of what is around us because we are full of plans for what lies ahead, or we are concerned over the past. It is amazing how few people can enjoy the now and give their full attention to what is around them. For living fully, it is important to extend your attention span, to be able to focus on the now and what is before you. A short attention span makes for shallow relationships, for poor perception and reception. This is true of our relationship with God as it is with each other.

The people who used this prayer made space in their lives. Note that this is a focusing prayer, that is a prayer to make us ready for deeper prayer. This turning to God at the opening of the day can transform our lives. Giving attention to God helps us to keep the world and all that happens in better focus. To think that the greatest power in the universe is offered to us and we are too busy to allow ourselves to become aware, it is hard to believe.

Come bend the knee: acknowledge the presence.

Know the Father, who created you and the whole universe, is with you.

Rejoice that he gives you life and all that is in the world around you.

Know that in him you live and move and have your being.

Become a friend of the Father and experience his love for you. It is no use rushing off words of prayer if you fail to get the beginning right. You might like to give him thanks each day for some part, some gift of his creation. Above all abide in his love and throughout the day affirm his presence.

Come to the Son who came that you might have life in all its fullness. Give thanks for the 'Word made flesh' that our God has come among us. Each day it is good to read a portion of one of the gospels and to rejoice in the life of Jesus Christ. Above all know him as the risen Lord and enjoy his presence and trust in his saving power. Know he still gives himself for you and to you in love.

Come to the Holy Spirit, the Lord and giver of life. Let the Spirit of God inspire you and renew your life. Rest in the Spirit and be refreshed by the Spirit. Know that the Spirit is at work through our talents and our abilities. Offer each task you have to do to the Spirit and seek that the Spirit will empower you.

Know the Holy Three are with you 'in friendship and affection'; say 'yes' to this relationship and let life be transformed.

Think on these words from Dag Hammarskjöld:

> At some moment I did answer 'Yes' to Someone – or Something – and from that hour I was certain that existence is meaningful and that, therefore, my life in self-surrender has a goal.
>
> (Dag Hammarskjöld, *Markings*, Faber and Faber, 1964, p. 205)

THE THREE

> In the name of the Father,
> In the name of the Son,
> In the name of the Spirit,
> Three in One:
>
> Father cherish me,
> Son cherish me,
> Spirit cherish me,
> Three all-kindly.
>
> God make me holy,
> Christ make me holy,
> Spirit make me holy,
>
> Three all-holy.
> Three aid my hope
> Three aid my love,
> Three aid my eye,
> And my knee from stumbling,
> My knee from stumbling.
> (*Carmina Gadelica* III, p. 63)

This is set down as a morning prayer, though it could fit any time of the day. It is another prayer that begins by affirming our immersion, our baptism. Perhaps in the days gone by this prayer would have been started with the signing of the cross as a reminder of the signing in our baptism and of the saving power of God. It is a good way still to begin this prayer. This is a wonderful example of extending a simple prayer. If we extend a prayer regularly then when it comes in its shorter form – even if reduced to 'God is here', or even to 'God' (could that ever be a reduction!) – it will still be vibrant with the fullness of our prayer. Too often our prayers fail to vibrate for we have never fully given them our attention and allowed the impact of their meaning to speak to us. Take time to let God into your life.

'In the name of the Father' is shorthand. Start, 'In the presence of the Father', be still and repeat it each time you wander from the presence. Know that God is with you. After a while continue, 'In the peace of the Father'; let the peace of God which passes all understanding come into your life. Open yourself to God's gift. You could move on to, 'In the power of the Father'. The creator of the universe, God, who holds all things in being offers you strength and power. Rest in the knowledge that you are not asked to achieve on your own, for God is with you.

Perhaps the first time you extend this prayer you should stay praying to the Father and enjoy being with him. There is no reason to move on quickly, you could stay with these opening words for weeks or years.

Another time move to; 'In the name of the Son': in the presence of the Christ who came down to lift you up; in the power of the Saviour who died that you should live; in the peace of the Holy One who triumphed over death and offers you life eternal; in the presence of the risen Lord who offers you his love. Know that this day you walk with Christ and Christ walks with you. Again take your time and affirm this reality. Use this way of opening your life to Jesus for days if not longer.

Then at some time move on to rejoice in the Spirit: in the power of the Spirit the Lord and giver of life; the Spirit who enables you and gives you himself as well as his gifts; the Spirit who is the breath of life; the Spirit who is about you and within you.

If you allow this reality to vibrate in your life then the words you use are full of meaning. The words now have greater content than mere words can convey. Now affirm that the Holy Three love you and make you holy. You are holy not because you are doing good or because you have said your prayers, but rather because you belong to God and God is with you. Holiness is not something that you achieve, it is God's gift of himself to you. You can reveal holiness by letting his presence be reflected in your life and what you do.

The important thing is to abide in him and let him abide in you.

When you abide in him God can far more easily come to your aid, for you have opened the way for him to enter. God often offers his help and aid but we are so unaware and we assume wrongly that God is far off. Turn to him and you will discover he is waiting to meet you. You will discover God is your hope, your love, your protection from falling.

THE SMOORING OF THE FIRE

The sacred Three
To save,
To shield,
To surround
The hearth,
The house,
The household,
This eve,
This night,
Oh! this eve,
This night,
And every night,
Each single night. Amen
(*Carmina Gadelica* I, p. 235)

For the smooring (smothering) of the fire:

> The embers are evenly spread on the hearth – which is generally in
> the middle of the floor – and formed into a circle. This circle is
> then divided into three equal sections, a small boss being left
> in the middle. A peat is laid between each section, each peat touch-
> ing the boss, which forms a common centre. The first peat is
> laid down in the name of the God of Life, the second in the name
> of the God of Peace, the third in the name of the God of Grace. The
> circle is then covered over with ashes sufficient to subdue but not
> extinguish the fire, in the name of the Three of Light.
>
> Then the woman of the house would close her eyes, stretch out
> her hands and offer the smooring prayer. So the day closes, as it
> began, in prayer to the Holy Trinity.
>
> (*Carmina Gadelica* I, pp. 234–5)

It is difficult to imagine the darkness in one of these highland
houses when the flame of the fire is smothered with ashes and
any other light extinguished. This can be a time of fear, a time
of danger.

Often in literature and art there are depictions of a dark night,
when lights are disappearing, the sun has gone and a greyness or
blackness descends. In the dark the mind can become bewildered,
confused. The night is the time for our own demons to assail us: a
time when we can lose our way and lose heart. Darkness is sym-
bolic of loss: it can be of hope or faith, a loss of employment or a
loved one; it can be failing health or the onset of frailty. All remind
us we are not almighty and we are perishable goods, our day comes
to an end. We must learn to face this reality because we cannot
escape it. If we pretend the darkness cannot come then it will over-
take us unprepared.

But this is only half the picture. It is like looking at a negative
when we should develop the whole picture. 'For God so loved the
world that he gave his only Son, so that everyone who believes in
him may not perish but may have everlasting life' (John 3.16). We
may have to face all sorts of disasters, darkness may suddenly
descend but in Christ Jesus we are not left in the dark. We know
the Son has risen and in him we have been offered eternal life. We
know that our God the creator of light is present and our God

loves us. Even when our faith weakens and our hope grows dim our God is a great God and he cares for us. Even when we lose our grip on God we are still in his hands and his love. Even when his voice is silent God is still with us.

The words and actions of this woman can form a good basis for a family to use as a prayer at the end of a day or as darkness descends. The night is not empty, for in it there is the friendliness and love of the Sacred Three. The family are not alone when darkness descends; the night is no longer an enemy. When the family lie down to sleep, the house, the hearth, the home are still in the presence. The presence does not depend on our consciousness or our awareness. God is not made to come to us by our prayers or our faith for he is ever present, even in the dark. Beneath the peats carefully laid out, the fire is not extinguished. Though the fire is hidden it is there and 'nothing can separate us from the love of God in Christ Jesus'.

This prayer is a good one for any family to pray at the end of a day or as darkness descends. A similar prayer is in the service of Compline and a prayer that I often pray at the end of a day:

> Be present, O merciful God,
> and protect us through the silent hours of this night,
> so that we who are wearied by the changes and chances
>   of this fleeting world,
> may rest upon your eternal changelessness:
> through Jesus Christ our Lord.
> **Amen.**
>
> *(Common Worship: Daily Prayer*,
> Church House Publishing, 2005, p. 345)

Or this prayer from Evening Prayer:

> Lighten our darkness,
> Lord, we pray, and in your great mercy
> defend us from all perils and dangers of this night,
> for the love of your only Son,
> our Saviour Jesus Christ.
> **Amen.**
>
> *(Common Worship: Daily Prayer*, p. 124)

I Arise Today

I ARISE TODAY

Thanks be to Thee, O God, that I have risen today,
To the rising of this life itself;
May it be to Thine own glory, O God of every gift,
And to the glory of my soul likewise.

O great God, aid Thou my soul
With the aiding of Thine own mercy;
Even as I clothe my body with wool,
Cover Thou my soul with the shadow of Thy wing.

Help me to avoid every sin,
And the source of every sin to forsake;
As the mist scatters on the crests of the hills,
May each ill haze clear from my soul, O God.
(*Carmina Gadelica* III, p. 31)

Do you start the day with acknowledging God's gift of life? There is a sense in which each day is a resurrection day. We rise from sleep to enter into the fullness of life and newness of life. Too often we enter a new day dragging all of our old troubles and fears with us. We do not give the newness of the day a chance to be a day of refreshment.

To start the day I often use the words of John Keble:

New every morning is the love
Our wakening and uprising prove;
Through sleep and darkness safely brought
Restored to life, and power, and thought.

New mercies, each returning day,
Hover around us while we pray;
New perils past, new sins forgiven,
New thoughts of God, new hopes of heaven.

Truly we arise to newness of life: each day is a resurrection day. If we do not believe in the resurrection it is obvious we have not spent any time with the risen Lord. We have failed to acknowledge his presence; we have not got to know him. So we miss out on the awareness of the power of his resurrection.

Learn to live the resurrection. Do not forever be looking backwards to the land of Palestine and what Jesus once did. Learn to walk with the risen Lord. Yes, it is important to know the Gospel stories but it is far more important to know the Christ who is alive. It is of little use to be able to recite the Scriptures if it is not a way of revealing the God who is, and letting the risen Lord come to us and touch our hearts. There is need to know about the empty tomb but we are not meant to keep returning there. We are to take to heart the words of St Luke, 'Why do you look for the living among the dead? He is not here, but has risen' (24.5). Perhaps it is no accident that there is no appearance of Christ in the tomb. He does not want us to be held by the grave and death, nor to concentrate our thoughts and energies there. When we are faced with the presence of the risen Lord, to spend our time looking into the tomb is foolishness. Make every day a resurrection day.

Walk with Christ, talk to him, break bread with him and share your life with him. Above all make sure you get to know him. Do not relegate him to the past, to history, for he is the living Lord.

To know the risen Lord is essential to your faith. Without this relationship your faith is meaningless. If he is not raised then there is no resurrection, or eternal life for us. Once you know the risen Lord all of life takes on a whole new meaning. You are no longer in the realm of dogma or theories, for you share life with the risen Lord; you discover life is now, not will be one day; life is eternal. St Jerome, in his commentary on the Psalms, said, 'Blessed are those in whose hearts Christ arises every day because every day such people are purged of their smallest sins.'

I have always been frightened by Miss Haversham in *Great Expectations* by Charles Dickens. She shut out the sun and turned her back on the present. She remained in the past, in a pain that she should have allowed to be healed. Her room was dark because she refused to let the light in. Do you let the Christ into your life and let him arise in your heart?

There is a wonderful section in *Common Worship: Daily Prayer*, entitled 'The Acclamation of Christ at the Dawning of the Day' (p. 108), which I use daily. Learn from it at least the words: 'May Christ the daystar dawn in our hearts and triumph over the shades of night.'

Sometimes I replace this with the words that are used at Easter: 'May the Christ risen in glory scatter the darkness from my heart and mind and from this world.'

Keep a 'resurrection day' each week, a day when you are truly elevated, lifted up out of the humdrum and into the Other. Seek to place yourself under the renewing power of him who makes all things new. Be open to this power, not to shut it out with activity and noise, but be still and know. All of this is not an escape from the world but an entering into it in great depth and with far greater resources. This is an entering into the Kingdom of God. Becoming part of the new creation (the eighth day). Remember that for the early Christians Sunday was the first day of the working week – not for 'Monday morning blues' but for arising to life and the tasks ahead. They wanted the power of the resurrection to be at work in all that was in their life and what lay ahead. Celebrate today as a resurrection day and say: 'Christ the daystar dawns in our hearts and defeats the darkness of night and death'.

IN THE POWER OF THE RISEN LORD

> I arise today
> Through the strength of Christ's birth with His baptism,
> Through the strength of His crucifixion with His burial,
> Through the strength of His resurrection with His ascension,
> Through the strength of His descent for the judgement of Doom.
> (attributed to St Patrick)

So many things would steal our life away from us. Sometimes we are just drained of energy and feel as if we are not fully alive. Recently I left my car in the drive with the rear window heater on for over three hours. On returning to the car the battery was completely drained of energy, there was not a bit of life in it. It was no use to keep trying – that would only make matters worse. It is a good workable car; it had plenty of petrol, but for all that it could not get going. It needed a power source from outside of itself to give it the spark of life. There are times when we all know this feeling in ourselves. There are times when we feel below par and we fail to achieve what we are truly capable of doing: we often fail to reach our potential. Sadly many have assumed that this is the normal way of life. Yet I am reminded of the words of Irenaeus writing in the second century: 'The glory of God is a man fully alive: and the life of man consists in beholding God.' True liveliness is not revealed by being 'party people', as enjoyable as that might be, but comes from knowing who made us and is with us. True liveliness involves a dimension to our lives that can only come from the Eternal. If this dimension is not awakened in us then we will continue to live below par, no matter how much we achieve. Jesus tells us that he came that we might have life and have it abundantly (John 10.10). It is in him and through him we come to that life which is eternal. Part of coming to the power source is to know of the earthly life of Jesus from his birth to his resurrection. It is good to spend time getting to know the Good News. Sadly so many Christians no longer know the story of their Saviour. But the story alone is not enough, for it is meant to be an introduction to the risen Lord. It is through knowing him we experience the power of his resurrection and are able to arise today to the fullness of life.

There is a story about a member of the Roman Legion who came to Caesar and asked that he might be allowed to commit suicide. The comment from his leader was, 'Man, I never knew that you were ever alive.' As a young child I lived in fear of becoming a 'zombie', one of the living dead! There is always the danger of us existing but not truly living. To this comes the challenge of the resurrection and the living Lord. One of the great attractions of Christianity is expressed for me by St Augustine: 'We are Easter people, alleluia is our song'.

Yet we need to acknowledge there is a great difference between saying we believe in the resurrection and in saying we know the risen Lord who is the resurrection. Without Jesus the idea of life beyond the grave is only a theory but with the risen Lord it becomes a reality and more it becomes part of our daily living. Not only do we express hope for the future but we arise this very day through Jesus Christ our Lord. Without the resurrection our faith is meaningless. If Jesus is not raised then there is no hope of eternal life. Once we know that Jesus lives, then all of life takes on a new meaning, and we have a new courage and hope. In his *Confessions*, St Patrick affirms this:

> I may pour out my life for His name's sake, even although myself may even be deprived of burial, and my corpse most miserably be torn limb from limb by dogs, or wild beasts, or that the fowls of the heaven devour it, I believe most certainly if this should happen to me, I shall have gained both body and soul. Because without any doubt we shall rise in that day in the brightness of the sun, that is in the glory of Christ our Redeemer, as sons of the living God, and joint heirs with Christ, and to be conformable to His image, for of Him and through Him and in Him we shall reign.
>
> (Charles H. H. Wright, *The Writings of St Patrick*,
> Religious Tract Society, pp. 70–1)

For the Christian, death is not the end but only a stopping place. Death may be terminal but the terminus is a halt on the journey where we get off to go somewhere else. When you alight at a rail or air terminus you have no intention of stopping there. In our journey through life the Celt had no doubt that whatever happened we are on our way to glory.

IN TUNE WITH CREATION

I arise today
Through the strength of heaven:
Light of sun,
Radiance of moon,

Splendour of fire,
Speed of lightning,
Swiftness of wind,
Depth of sea,
Stability of earth,
Firmness of rock.
(Eleanor Hull (ed.), *The Poem Book of the Gael*,
tr. Kuno Meyer, Chatto and Windus, 1913)

'Ecology' and 'holistic' may be relatively new words but what they call upon us to be aware of is as old as our understanding of the earth. We are part of this world and to harm the world is to do harm to ourselves. Columbanus, living in the sixth and seventh centuries, wrote: 'He who tramples on the earth tramples on himself.' One of the dangers of urban living is that it separates our thinking, and our hearts, from our roots. We do not feel as attached to the earth as earlier generations. In our insensitivity to the earth we have polluted rivers, over-fished our oceans, and destroyed great tracts of forests which influence the air we breathe. In disturbing the balance of nature we are in danger of making the world hostile to human life. We need to realize the world is actually held in a wonderful balance and we must do all that is in our power to maintain that balance. I find it rather sad when people give the impression that this world does not matter. God made this world out of his love and for his love. He did not make the world to condemn it but to pour his love upon it and be present within it. God placed us in the world that we might reflect his love for the world and in doing so give our love to him. If we are to praise the Creator we have to work in harmony with his creation. We cannot say we love the Maker of all, if we are disregarding the balance and the fragility of the earth that he has given to us.

The Celtic Christians saw and reflected a glory which we seem to have lost from the earth. Because of their faith they saw all things as interrelated and interdependent and that God is there in the midst of them. Because the world belongs to God and all that is in it there is a oneness, a unity that God gives. We, in our desire to dominate and control, seem to have lost sight of this unity. So many people no longer live as part of the greater whole; they live as if what they do does not affect us all. We should learn to say with the Psalmist: 'The earth is the Lord's and all that is in it, the world and those that live in it; for he has founded it on the seas, and established it on the rivers' (Psalm 24.1–2).

There is a great need to recapture that awareness which gives a holistic approach to all of life and all that exists. At the moment, so many seem not only out of tune with God but out of tune with the world and even with themselves. In his book, *The Tree of Life*, H. J. Massingham wrote: 'If the British Church had survived, it is possible the fissure between Christianity and nature, widening through the centuries, would not have cracked the unity of western man's attitude to the universe.'

After St Patrick acknowledges he depends on God for his being, he is able to turn his attention to the sun, the moon and the earth, the air and the seas. He affirms that he can only arise today because of these created things and their stability. He has no fear in doing this for God has created it so.

In our rising to life we need to look with new eyes on the life around us and let our heart go out to God's wonderful creation. Look upon the world. See yourself part of its wonderful order. Say with Julian of Norwich her three truths about the world:

The first is God made it.
The second is God loves it.
The third is that God looks after it.

(Julian of Norwich, *Enfolded in Love*, Darton, Longman and Todd, 1980, p. 3)

Rejoice that God is the Maker, the Lover and the Keeper of the world. Do not just take these words as facts, make them part of your experience of living in this world. Once or twice a week spend some time looking closely at some created thing. All of creation contains mystery if we look deep enough. If we look long enough and with our heart God's glory is waiting to be found in even the smallest of things. Meister Eckhart in the fourteenth century said: 'Every single creature is full of God and is about God.' If our senses were fully alert like Blake's we would be able:

To see a World in a Grain of Sand,
And Heaven in a Wild Flower,
Hold Infinity in the palm of your hand,
And Eternity in an hour.
(William Blake, 'Auguries of Innocence', *c.* 1803)

To the use of our senses the Celts often added what is sometimes known as the sixth sense, the heart. Many who teach the faith have taught how we need to see the world with 'the eyes of the heart'. Ask yourself how you look at the world: is it a place of wonder and love? Do you rise each day to the newness of life and the mystery of all that is about you? Take time to think about this. Perhaps you would like to think upon the words of that great scientist Albert Einstein:

Whoever is devoid of the capacity of wonder, whoever remains unmoved, whoever cannot contemplate or know the deep shudder of the soul in enchantment, might just as well be dead for he has already closed his eyes upon life.
(Michael Mayne, *This Sunrise of Wonder*, Fount, 1995, p. 109)

RISING PRAYER

Bless to me, O God,
Each thing mine eye sees;
Bless to me, O God,
Each sound mine ear hears;
Bless to me, O God,
Each odour that goes into my nostrils;
Bless to me, O God,
Each taste that goes into my lips,
Each note that goes into my song,
Each ray that guides my way,
Each thing that I pursue,
Each lure that tempts my will,

The zeal that seeks my living soul,
The Three that seek my heart,
The zeal that seeks my living soul,
The Three that seek my heart.
(*Carmina Gadelica* III, p. 33)

One of the great accounts of awakening is the story of Jacob after he left his home at Beersheba on a journey to Paddan-aram to find a wife among his relatives. As the sun set, Jacob took a stone for a pillow, put it under his head and lay down to sleep. That night he had a dream of angels descending and ascending to heaven and the voice of God speaking to him. In the morning he awoke out of sleep and said, 'Surely the Lord is in this place and I did not know it!' He was truly awake and he saw the world as he never saw it before. He was full of awe and wonder, and said, 'How awesome is this place! This is none other than the house of God, and this is the gate of heaven.' Before leaving the place he gave it a new name, Bethel, 'the House of God'. (Read Genesis 28.10–22.) Jacob learned that God is, and that God is with us.

His eyes were truly opened and he saw that God was not far away but to be met with in our journey and on this earth. Once this discovery is made faith awakens and a relationship with the living God begins. Sadly most of us rarely open our eyes. Our senses are dulled and we do not respond in wonder to the world around us. We fail to recognize that this is God's creation and that our God speaks to us through our senses and our heart.

The Celtic peoples talked of the Primary Scriptures. They believed that you could not fully understand the depth of the New Testament unless you had some knowledge of the Old Testament. They would add to this that you could not understand the Old Testament unless you understood the Primary Scriptures. The Primary Scriptures are the way we see and read the world. It is no use reading books if you are illiterate in the reading of the world. If you are insensitive to the things that are around you, how can you hope to be sensitive to the unseen God? If you are uncaring towards creation how can you express care for its Creator? We learn of the mystery of God through the mystery of creation. There is great depth in the words of Columbanus:

Who, I say, shall explore His highest summit to the measure of His unutterable and inconceivable being? Who shall examine the secret depths of God? Who shall dare to treat of the eternal source of the universe? Who shall boast of knowing the infinite God, Who fills all and surrounds all, Who enters into all and passes beyond all, Who occupies all and escapes all? Whom none has seen as He is. Therefore let no man venture to seek out the unsearchable things of God, the nature, mode and cause of His existence. These are unspeakable, undiscoverable, unsearchable; only believe in simplicity and yet with firmness, that God is and shall be even as He has been, since God is immutable . . . Understand the creation, if you wish to know the Creator.

> (Walker, G. S. M., ed., *Sancti Columbani Opera*,
> The Dublin Institute for Advanced Studies, 1970, p. 65)

To help in this approach to God the Celt asked to be sensitive to what is around him or her. They talk of playing the 'five-stringed harp' which is the five senses. If our senses are not used properly our approach to God can be distorted. God speaks to us through our senses. We should not only affirm the presence but delight in it with all our senses. Our whole being should vibrate with delight in God who is ever near. Seek to discover that the place on which you stand is 'holy ground'. You might like to begin by saying with Jacob, 'Surely the Lord is in this place – and I did not know it!' Or to affirm with Jacob, 'How awesome is this place! This is none other than the house of God, and this is the gate of heaven' (Genesis 28.16, 17).

To be unaware of this is to be insensitive and is the beginning of death. Writing in his journal, Dag Hammarskjöld wrote:

God does not die on the day when we cease to believe in a personal deity, but we die on the day when our lives cease to be illumined by the steady radiance, renewed daily, of a wonder, the source of which is beyond all reason.

> (Dag Hammarskjöld, *Markings*, Faber and Faber, 1964, p. 64)

JESU WHO OUGHT TO BE PRAISED

It were as easy for Jesu
To renew the withered tree
As to wither the new
Were it His will so to do.
Jesu! Jesu! Jesu!
Jesu! meet it were to praise Him.

There is no plant in all the ground
But is full of His virtue,
There is no form in the strand
But is full of His blessing,
Jesu! Jesu! Jesu!
Jesu! meet it were to praise Him.

There is no life in the sea,
There is no creature in the river,
There is naught in the firmament,
But proclaims His goodness.
Jesu! Jesu! Jesu!
Jesu! meet it were to praise Him.

There is no bird on the wing,
There is no star in the sky,
There is nothing beneath the sun,
But proclaims His goodness.
Jesu! Jesu! Jesu!
Jesu! meet it were to praise Him.
    (*Carmina Gadelica* I, pp. 39–41)

We are told that this prayer was said by a woman on Harris Island who had leprosy. She had been made to leave her community and to dwell alone on the sea-shore, where she lived off plants and shellfish. She bathed herself in the liquid in which she boiled the plants. All her sores became healed and her flesh became new – possibly as a result of the action of the plants and shellfish. A cottar living at Bunessan on the Mull affirmed, 'The Being of life never set a thing in the creation of the universe but he set some good within it – He never did. O King, many a good is in the soil of the earth and in the depth of the sea, did we but know to make

41

good use of them – many, many a good, O Thou perfect King of life'. However her healing came about, it must have made a wonderful difference to the life of the woman with leprosy.

Leprosy and the fear of it were common in medieval times. The lepers were often driven from their home and loved ones, and they were accounted as good as dead. In fact in the Middle Ages the burial service was said over lepers as they were sent away from their community. The loneliness and separation from loved ones must have been extremely hard to bear. Even today one of the worst punishments a person can endure is prolonged solitary confinement. Yet this woman was not totally alone for she was able to turn to God in prayer. She trusted in Jesus and prayed to him. She was aware that the risen Lord had the power to give newness of life, to give life to 'a withered tree'. She asked the risen Lord to help her to arise from the 'living death' and to newness of flesh and life. As we cannot be split into body, mind and spirit, for we are one being, we cannot belittle the relationship with the risen Lord in her healing. It would seem from this prayer that she was used to calling upon 'Jesu! Jesu! Jesu!' as her risen Lord.

The Jesus Prayer may begin on the lips as a call. But it has to enter our mind and we need to know upon whom we are calling. We have to centre our minds on him. The woman does this by acknowledging that 'There is no plant in all the ground but is full of his virtue.' Nor was there anything that was not full of his blessing. Jesus offered himself to her through the world in which she lived. The fish of the sea, the birds of the air, all that is in the earth and the stars of the sky reminded her of his goodness. This is not a case of pantheism but rather an example of one who loved the risen Lord and was reminded of him through creation, as a person is reminded of a loved one through a photograph or a token. She sees the world full of the blessing and goodness of Jesus. This is not a request for the presence but rather an affirmation of its reality. Once aware of the risen Lord, that awareness affects our whole being and the world around us. The prayer becomes a prayer of the heart, of love to love.

Few words in love are far better than many words without depth. You may like to use the 'Jesus Prayer' as used in the

Orthodox Church and by many other Christians. 'Jesus, Son of the living God, have mercy upon me a sinner.' Say it first with the lips, then with the mind and then with the heart.

There is a lovely statement of this way of praying to Jesus in *Franny and Zooey* by J. D. Salinger:

> 'If you keep saying that prayer over and over again', says Franny, '– you will just have to do it with your lips at first – then eventually something happens, and the words get synchronized with the person's heart-beats, and then you are actually praying without ceasing.'

When this happens you are able to know that you work and walk in the presence of the risen Lord. You find him in the garden, by the sea shore, behind locked doors, at a meal or on a mountain, just as the disciples did of old. You know that you are not alone in the world and not left to cope without divine help. Then you can join those of whom it is said, 'Then were the disciples glad when they saw the Lord.'

Often I use only his name, Jesus, the name that means saviour or deliverer. He waits to hear your call, to be invited into your life. Speak to Jesus, say his name with your lips, speak it out, let it vibrate on the air and in your ears. Let his name be often on your tongue. Say it quietly with each breath. Do not try to imagine Jesus. At the beginning do not even try and think about what you are saying. Just call his name.

Now use your mind, continue to call upon Jesus, but seek to acknowledge that he is with you. The risen Lord comes to you. Know him as your friend, your Saviour and your God. Rejoice and rest in his presence. Know he says to you 'Lo I am with you always'.

The mind cannot fully comprehend this: let it enter your heart. Give your love to him and abide in his love. Call his name from the depth of your heart and invite him to come to you. Rest in his love. Let his love surround you and fill you. Learn to rejoice in the Lord always. Continue to say his name in love until you can say with the disciples who were on the road to Emmaus, 'Were not our hearts burning within us while he was talking to us on the road?' (Luke 24.32)

Working and Walking with the Creator

ALL BELONGS TO GOD

Each day I remember the source of the mercies
Thou hast bestowed upon me gently and generously;
Each day may I be fuller in love to Thyself.

Each thing I have received, from Thee it came,
Each thing for which I hope, from Thy love it will come,
Each thing I enjoy, it is of Thy bounty,
Each thing I ask, come of Thy disposing
Holy God, loving Father, of the word everlasting,
Grant me to have of Thee this living prayer:
Lighten my understanding, kindle my will, begin my doing,
Incite my love, strengthen my weakness, enfold my desire.

(Carmina Gadelica III, p. 59)

Work is no less presence-filled than church worship. The ploughing of a field or milking a cow is as holy as kneeling in prayer. To make one greater than the other is to fall into dualism that tends to separate God and his world. We need to affirm God comes with the territory, in reality it is the territory which comes with God. For the Celtic mind the creation speaks of God and introduces us to God. God may transcend our knowledge or our awareness, he may be beyond our mental comprehension but he is not separate from us. The transcendence of God is not about distance, it is not a spatial separation but rather about the greatness of his being which no created thing can fully contain. The God who transcends all our knowledge can still be comprehended by our hearts, by love.

There is a sense in which the daily prayers of the Celts, when about their work, truly reveal their awareness of the presence and love of God. The shepherd is as much in the presence of God with his sheep as he is when he comes to a church building; the woman bowed in milking or over her loom is as bowed before God as she would be in church worship. The fishermen rejoice in God's presence on the sea as much as they do in the sacraments. God is not divided into places of sacred and secular. The Celtic Christians lived their faith by continually turning to the presence and love of God. This is a great challenge to all who compartmentalize God and give only a realm, which they choose to call sacred, to God and worship. Nothing, no task or person is outside his presence. We need to learn again to see God in the world and the world in God. He is where we are at this moment. You may like to stop here and rejoice that the Lord is with you.

There is always a danger of calling the Celts pantheists simply because we have relegated God to part of life. But we must ask ourselves, is God not in all things? If there are some things in which God is not present then he is less than God. It is fashionable to talk rather of pan-en-theist to emphasize that all is in God. This is very true but we must not lose sight of the fact that he dwells within his world and that we dwell in him and he in us. Our lives and the great mysteries of the universe, the mystery of God himself are all interwoven like some great Celtic carpet pattern, with each thing touching and being part of another. We can experience at any moment what Gerard Manley Hopkins says of the world in his poem 'God's Grandeur':

> The world is charged with the grandeur of God,
> It will flame out, like shining from shook foil.

Never believe that the world or humankind has lost its glory, the presence of God has not left it. The glory may be somewhat tarnished in our eyes but it is there and waits to be revealed. If we follow the crowds, if we fill our lives with sounds, we may never see, hear or be aware of the wonder and glory. If we thrust out a little each day, making time and space, there are great wonders to behold. Learn to do little things for the love of God and rejoice he is with you. Brother Lawrence said, 'It is enough for me to pick up but a straw from the ground for the love of God'. By turning to God even the most tedious of labours can be transformed. This does not come from some rural idyll but from a people whose lives were hard and often spent in poverty and hunger. But these lives were God-filled lives, lives transformed by his glory.

This discovery of the presence of God is to see all things in their depth and in their beauty. If we ignore the presence that vibrates in every atom then we live a lie, we become lonely and alone with a deep sense of loss. If everyone around us shares that same loss we are in danger of accepting that loss for normality. Think deeply on these words:

> God speaks to man through the things and beings he sends into a man's life: man answers by the ways in which he deals with these same things. (Martin Buber)

And:

> God regards not the greatness of the work, but the love which prompts it.
>
> (Brother Lawrence, *Spiritual Maxims*, H. R. Allenson, 1906, p. 36)

THE WILL OF GOD

> God's will I would do,
> My own will bridle;
> God's due I would give,
> My own due yield;
> God's path I would travel,
> My own path refuse;
> Christ's death I would ponder,
> My own death remember;
> Christ's agony would I meditate,
> My love to God make warmer;
> (*Carmina Gadelica* III, p. 51)

This prayer reminds me of my training for the priesthood. The main aim of the Society of the Sacred Mission who taught me was, 'To give glory to God in doing his will'. In the Principles of the Society it was said: 'God is glorified when his will is done. Some fulfil it by patience and prayer, some in teaching, some in labour.' Further on we were directed, 'Find your pleasure in doing his will, and beholding his glory.'

If we have any awareness of God at all it demands a reaction from us. To be unaware of God or of spiritual things means we are less than human, for we were created for this to know God and to do his will. This will is not the will of a tyrant but rather of a loving Father who seeks the best for us. To seek to do his will makes us approach our work and our life in a special way. It is not the action of a slave but of one who works out of love and in co-operation with the God of love. We discover we can share in his redeeming love for the whole of creation. When describing how a person should please God, Columbanus said in a sermon:

> What is the best thing in the world? To please the Creator. What is his will? To fulfil what he commanded, that is, to live rightly and dutifully to seek the Eternal; for duty and justice are the will of Him who is dutiful and right.
>
> (*Sancti Columbani Opera*, G. S. M. Walker, Dublin, p. 73)

In a Catechism that is attributed to St Ninian we learn of the deep desire to do God's will.

Question	What is best in this world?
Answer	To do the will of our Maker.
Question	What is his will?
Answer	That we should live according to the laws of his creation.
Question	How do we know those laws?
Answer	By study – study the Scriptures with devotion.
Question	What tool has our Maker provided for this study?
Answer	The intellect which can probe everything.
Question	And what is the fruit of study?
Answer	To perceive the eternal Word of God reflected in every plant and insect, every bird and animal, and every man and woman.

> (Robert Van de Weyer, *Celtic Fire*, Darton, Longman and Todd, 1990, p. 96)

It is not lack of resources or time that holds us back from serving God; it is our own volition, our will power. Too often we fail to make a definite choice and just drift from one thing to another. In this drifting, we tend to ignore the presence and the love of God and let whatever impinges upon us occupy us. Long ago the prophet Elijah saw that the danger for most people is that they do not definitely give themselves to God and his glory, or definitely deny him, they just haver between the two. He asked, 'How long will you go limping with two different opinions? If the LORD is God follow him' (1 Kings 18.21). If we say we believe in God it should show in the way we live, in our actions and in our desire to serve him.

We decide whom or what we will serve, and who we will become, by the choices we make or do not make. If we make comfort and money our goal we will put our energies and abilities into these enterprises. We will measure our life by how much comfort we have achieved and how much money we have collected. If you have ceased to pray daily, you must ask yourself the reason why? If you are bored with God, it is not that God is boring. The Creator of the universe, the Giver of life, the Lord risen from the dead cannot be boring. Your approach to God can be boring. You have made your God too small by not giving him the attention due. Stop and think over these words from Brother Lawrence:

Believe me, count as lost each day you have not used in loving God.
(*Spiritual Maxims*, p. 52)

Once you decide to seek God and his will properly you will be called to adventure upon adventure. You will not be saved from the troubles of this world but you will know Who goes with you and cares for you, for your God is always there wherever you are. The Celtic people showed that even the dullest work can be transformed by seeking to do it as an act of love to God and to his glory. Think over these words of George Herbert and see if you can fulfil them in your daily life:

Teach me, my God and King,
in all things Thee to see;
and what I do in anything
to do it as for Thee . . .

49

A servant with this clause
makes drudgery divine;
who sweeps a room, as for thy laws,
makes that and the action fine.
(George Herbert, 'The Elixir')

THE GLORY OF GOD

Even though the day be laden and my task dreary, and my strength
small, a song keeps singing in my heart. For I know that I am Thine.
I am part of Thee. Thou art kin to me and all times are in Thy hand.
(Alistair Maclean, *Hebridean Altars*,
Hodder & Stoughton, 1999, p. 30)

It is easy to romanticize the life of the Hebridean crofter. In reality
much of it was hard graft for little reward. Very often they did well
to survive, especially in hard winters. Much work was repetitive
and for some involved great dangers. There were times when the
people were often near to starvation level. Yet they were a people
of song, they learnt to rejoice in what was around them and more,
they rejoiced in the glory of God. This song came from the depth
of their heart as it was a song of love towards God in response to
the love they had received from him.

Often a crofter family lived in greater solitude that many a
monastic establishment and with greater deprivation. At least the
space did give them time to turn to God. In their solitude they
did not experience the loneliness of many people in a society full
of people. Their lives were not empty for they were presence-filled.
They knew they belonged. They belonged to the world in which
they lived and they belonged to God. Because they turned to God
in love they could face the direst circumstances with hope and with
courage. They believed that even when life seemed to go against
them their loving God still had and would keep the ultimate control. The final outcome is always in God's hands and power and
'nothing can separate us from the love of God in Christ Jesus'.

These people did not simply accept their lot, they strove to improve it and to transform it, but above all they found the love of God and his glory within it. They wove more than a song into their lives; they wove the awareness of the Almighty. Their prayer often had a great simplicity: they did not question God's presence, nor did they just assume it, they got to know God and this brought into their lives a glory.

If there is to be any real and lasting glory in your life, remember it comes from him and is his. I still remember in my student days being given an essay on 'The Glory of God'. I looked up the meaning of 'glory' in Greek and Hebrew. There was much about the hidden presence of God. I then turned to look up 'glory' in the *Theological Word Book*. It simply said, 'See God'. I knew it was referring me to another page but I closed the book for I had been given what I was looking for: if you want to know glory, see God! See God in all that you do. See his presence in the world. See him in the other person who comes to you. See and know that God never leaves you. All this seeing is done with the 'eyes of the heart'.

Let his presence put song into your heart – as the spiritual says:

> Oh you gotta get a glory
> In the work that you do,
> A Halleluiah chorus,
> In the heart of you,
> Paint or tell a story,
> Sing or shovel coal,
> But you gotta get a glory
> Or the job lacks soul.

BLESSING

> Bless to me, O God,
> The earth beneath my foot
> Bless to me, O God,

The path whereon I go;
Bless to me, O God,
The thing of my desire;
Thou Evermore of evermore,
Bless thou to me my rest.

Bless to me the thing
Whereon I set my mind,
Bless to me the thing
Whereon I set my love;
Bless to me the thing
Whereon I set my hope;
O Thou King of kings,
Bless thou to me mine eye!
(*Carmina Gadelica* III, p. 181)

The reciter of this prayer told how he spoke it 'under his breath' when he went on a journey, however short the distance, however small the errand. We need to remember that for travellers of earlier times every journey could be fraught with danger. Most of these people had never travelled more than twenty miles from home and some much less than that. To travel any distance meant to leave behind home and loved ones, security and a means of livelihood. The community around a person gave them safety and protection as well as fellowship. To go away from home was to go into the unknown, into the unpredictable. Away from your own community you not only had no standing or purpose but you were looked upon as a nameless person and an alien. In leaving home you could take little with you, as travel was likely to be on foot and you could only take what you could carry. At nights you would find yourself without shelter and all alone. Yet travellers were not alone for they had a companion on the way: they walked with God and God went with them. In a prayer we shall soon look at what Columba says:

'Alone with none but Thee, my God,
I journey on my way.'

This reminds me of the time when the attendant of Elisha panicked when he arose early and saw that they were surrounded by an enemy's army. When he asked what they should do, Elisha replied, 'Do not be afraid, for there are more with us than there are with them.' Elisha then prayed that his attendant might have 'eyes to see'. When the servant's eyes were truly opened he saw that there was a far greater power with them and there was no need for fear (see 2 Kings 6.15–17).

These travellers might not be sure of what lay ahead but they knew who went with them. They did not have the loneliness of many modern travellers for they were aware of the presence and the love of God and they could converse with their God on the way. In many ways they took to heart what was told them in the Scriptures:

> Do not fear, for I have redeemed you:
> I have called you by your name, you are mine.
> When you pass through the waters, I will be with you . . .
> when you walk through fire you shall not be burned . . .
> For I am the LORD your God, the Holy One of Israel, your
>   Saviour.
>
> (Isaiah 43.1–3)

To be aware of the presence is to be blessed, to be strengthened and encouraged in your journey. To have a companion to share your troubles is to have them eased, especially when the companion is the Almighty. Into the life of such a person comes the knowledge that in the love of God in the end all will be well, for in God life is eternal.

Today we often travel cocooned by a car with the heater or the air conditioning on. We have a map or a Sat Nav for guidance. We tune in to some programme or play music of our choice. Yet none of this protects us from loneliness or from long-term, if not immediate, dangers. The Celtic Christian was aware of his final destination and with God's grace he would arrive there. He knew his final destination and Who would meet him there. In this he was truly blessed.

JOURNEYING

> Relieve Thou, O God, each
> In suffering on land or sea,
> In grief or wounded or weeping
> And lead them to the house of Thy peace
> This night.
>
> I am weary, weak and cold,
> I am weary of travelling land and sea,
> I am weary of traversing moorland and billow,
> Grant me peace in the nearness of Thy repose.
> This night . . .
>
> . . . To be resting with Jesus
> In the dwelling of peace.
>
> (*Carmina Gadelica* III, p. 177)

There is a restlessness and a Divine restlessness. St Augustine recognized long ago, 'O God, you have made us for yourself, and our heart is restless till it finds rest in you'. There is a restlessness that comes from our need for adventure and our feeling that there 'is more to life than this'. The divine restlessness comes from this and more, for it is also seeking to heed the call of God and to do his will.

I find it very interesting that many of the Celtic saints, usually in mid-life, decide to move out from the comfort and safety of their communities. Many of the Celtic saints sought to live this way, and to journey towards the Promised Land of God and deeper into God. Of the Welsh saint, Brynach, it was said: 'By thinking nothing of the place of his birth, by forsaking his own land, he sought to find it; by living in exile he hoped to reach home.'

For the Desert Fathers and the Celtic Christians the story of Abraham leaving Ur of the Chaldees became an image and model of doing God's will and adventure. The following is said to be part of a sermon by St Columba:

> God counselled Abraham to leave his own country and go in pilgrimage into the land which God had shown him, to wit the 'Land of Promise' – Now the good counsel which God had enjoined here on the father of the faithful is incumbent on all the faithful, that is

to leave their country and their land, their wealth and their worldly delight for the sake of the Lord of the Elements, and go in perfect pilgrimage in imitation of Him.

(Nora Chadwick, *Age of the Saints in the
Early Celtic Church*, OUP, 1961, p. 64)

People like Columba or Columbanus were men of position in their communities. They were respected and looked up to. Cuthbert was a leader in the Church, but each chose to move out into the unknown, where they were unknown. Columbanus went to Europe, Columba to Iona, Cuthbert to Inner Farne. If asked why, the answer could be quite simple: 'for the love of God'.

There is a lovely story in the Anglo-Saxon Chronicle of three Irishmen who landed in Cornwall after having crossed the sea in a boat made of hides and without oars. When they were asked in the presence of King Alfred of Wessex why they had come they replied, 'We stole away because we wanted for the love of God to be on pilgrimage, we cared not where'. The seeking of a desert in the ocean and the desire to go on pilgrimage for the love of God reflects the same yearning to extend one's life and to find not only meaning but one's true home. It is not surprising that the Irish, who lived on the 'edge of the world', were a nation who were forever reaching out into the beyond. In a sense, the beyond was always on their doorstep and now and again people were accidentally drawn into it. If people came from the 'back of beyond' with a story of what they had seen, adventurers would want to go there and even further. What the pilgrim seeks is not a new territory but a new spiritual depth, a beyond in our midst. Every true pilgrimage is not only an outward journey but a journey inwards and we all have great depths to discover within ourselves. Pilgrimage is not a journey to God but a journey with God and in God. It is good to learn to journey for the 'love of God'.

In your journey through life take to heart these words of Julian of Norwich:

> Would you know your Lord's meaning in this? Learn it well. Love was his meaning. Who showed it to you? Love. Why did he show it to you? For love. Hold fast to this, and you shall learn and know

more about love, but you will never need to know or understand about anything else for ever and ever. Thus did I learn that love was our Lord's meaning.

(Julian of Norwich, *Enfolded in Love*, Darton,
Longman and Todd, 1980, p. 59)

What Shall I Fear?

WHAT SHALL I FEAR?

HELMSMAN   Blest be the boat.
CREW   God the Father bless her.
HELMSMAN   Blest be the boat.
CREW   God the Son bless her.
HELMSMAN   Blest be the boat.
CREW   God the Spirit bless her.
ALL   God the Father,
            God the Son,
            God the Spirit,
            Bless the boat.
HELMSMAN   What can befall you
            And God the Father with you?
CREW   No harm can befall us.
HELMSMAN   What can befall you
            And God the Son with you?
CREW   No harm can befall us.
HELMSMAN   What can befall you
            And God the Spirit with you?
CREW   No harm can befall us.
ALL   God the Father,
            God the Son,
            God the Spirit,
            With us eternally.
HELMSMAN   What can cause you anxiety
            And the God of the elements over you?
CREW   No anxiety can be ours.
HELMSMAN   What can cause you anxiety
            And the King of the elements over you?
CREW   No anxiety can be ours.
HELMSMAN   What can cause you anxiety
            And the Spirit of the elements over you?
CREW   No anxiety can be ours.

ALL The God of the elements,
The King of the elements,
The Spirit of the elements,
Close over us,
Ever eternally.

(*Carmina Gadelica* I, p. 333)

The Hebridean fishermen set out knowing the great dangers of the sea. Where the Atlantic beats against the islands there are some of the most dangerous seas in the world. These were men who lived at the edge of the world – and there was always the danger of going over the edge. They went out with holy water on their boat and with prayers and blessing, yet they knew they would not be able to avoid the storms and the danger of being overwhelmed. They were well aware that, as they used to say, the 'sea is so large and their boat so small'.

But to this is added the awareness that God is with them in the storm. They are not alone; God is alongside giving them strength, hope and the courage to be. Because of their faith they are able to venture. They are not left to fate. Even death is not fatal!! For nothing can separate us from the love of God in Christ Jesus. They may lose control but the storm is not in control for God is in control of our lives. The storm will pass, and we will live on in the fullness of life eternal.

On Holy Island I regularly looked at the notice boards for rescues performed by the lifeboat crew. These were often rescues in very dangerous seas and at the risk of life. Sometimes the notice only said 'stood by and gave help' and at other times it only said 'stood by'. Little words but what a difference that extra presence made on a stormy sea. Knowing they were not alone and that there was help at hand helped many a crew to ride out a storm or with escort make it safely to harbour. How often hearts were made strong by knowing they were not left to fate. This often brought to my mind the words of the hymn:

> Jesu, lover of my soul,
> let me to thy bosom fly,
> while the gathering waters roll,
> while the tempest still is high:

hide me, O my Saviour, hide,
till the storm of life is past;
safe into the haven guide,
O receive my soul at last.
 (Charles Wesley, 1707–1788)

A friend of mine describes such hymns and sentiments as escapist. But I tell him that they are not about escape but about having the sense to know where our strength and safety lie. In reality these verses hold two things together. First is that everyone will face troubles and storms. No one in this life can escape at least some dangers and the more adventurous you are the more dangers you are likely to face. There are some storms you will not survive on your own. To escape all dangers means you have never lived! The second is that our God comes down to where we are. We are not alone. And even when we are overwhelmed and the boat sinks, for us it is not the end. Nothing can separate us from the love of God in Christ Jesus.

Spend some time with these words from Julian of Norwich:

> He did not say, 'You shall not be tempest-tossed, you shall not be work-weary, you shall not be discomforted.' But he said, 'You shall not be overcome.' God wants us to heed these words so that we shall always be strong in trust, both in sorrow and joy.
>
> (Julian of Norwich, *Enfolded in Love*,
> Darton, Longman and Todd, 1980, p. 39)

CONFIDENCE IN GOD

Alone with none but Thee, my God,
I journey on my way;
What need I fear, when Thou art near,
O King of night and day?
More safe I am within Thy hand,
than if a host did round me stand.

> My destined time is fixed by Thee,
> and death doth know his hour.
> Did warriors strong around me throng,
> they could not stay his power;
> no walls of stone can man defend
> when Thou Thy messenger dost send.
>
> My life I yield to Thy decree,
> and bow to Thy control
> in peaceful calm, for from Thine arm
> no power can wrest my soul.
> Could earthly omens e'er appal
> A man that heeds the heavenly call!
>
> The child of God can fear no ill,
> His chosen dread no foe;
> we leave our fate with Thee and wait
> Thy bidding when we go.
> 'Tis not from chance our comfort springs,
> Thou art our trust, O King of kings.
>   (Columba, 521–97, translator unknown)

There is something wonderful about a football crowd singing, 'You'll never walk alone'. If only they made the words their experience. The sad thing is the words are often sung without much thought to their meaning. The words in fact are meaningless unless you believe in and experience the presence of God. The whole of the gospel story with the resurrection of Jesus needs to be known, or at least the presence of the risen Lord for the words to be truly dependable. It is true, we are not left on our own for our God is with us. We are in his presence and in his love no matter what happens in this world. One of the great expressions of this presence from the Old Testament is in Psalm 23 where the Lord is not only our shepherd but he will lead us through the dark valley of death. The Lord as our companion is our protector and our assurance that we will not be allowed to perish. Spend a little time reading and affirming each verse of Psalm 23.

Our faith does not save us from dangers or troubles but God does promise us that we will survive beyond it all. Such knowledge should give us the ability to live with confidence: *con fideo*, that is 'with faith'. Faith is not a matter of belief in God but rather relationship with God. Faith is knowing that God loves us and cares for us whatever the circumstance. Though on our side this relationship may waver, we may lose our grip, God does not leave us. God never loses his grip on us, though we can fail to be aware of it or ignore it. Our lives are enriched when we learn to rejoice in this presence and to put our trust in our God. We need to learn to put our hand in the hand of God. Quite often it is hard to bear a trouble or face a danger if we are alone – but we are never alone for our God is with us. We are never God-forsaken for God loves us. It is God alone that can be our deliverer from death. We cannot face death with any hope or confidence unless we trust in God and his almighty power. Eternal life is not something we gain or earn, it is a gift from God through his Son Christ our Lord.

You cannot grow in confidence if you do not make this relationship with God. You need to learn to talk to God each day and during the day. Do not make God only available at prayer time; have recourse to him during your work and on your travels. Seek to do work with him and to do his will. Be open to his glory that is in the world and rejoice in his creation. See your life as a pilgrimage that journeys deeper and deeper into the love of God. When we come to know the presence we are able to hold our head up high and not be afraid of the dark. We may not know what lies ahead but we do know who goes with us and who is ready to meet us at the end of the journey. It is not what we believe but who we believe in. Heed these wise words from Brother Lawrence:

> We cannot escape the dangers which abound in life, without the actual and continual help of God; let us then pray to Him for it continually. How can we pray to Him, without being with Him? How can we be with Him, but in thinking of Him often? And how can we often have Him in our thoughts, unless by holy habit of thought which we should form? You will tell me that I am always saying the same thing: it is true, for this is the easiest and best method that I know; and as I use no other, I advise the whole world to. We must *know* before we can *love*. In order to *know* God we must often *think* of Him; and when we come to *love* Him, we shall

also think of Him often, *for our heart will be with our treasure!*
Ponder over this often, ponder it well.

(Brother Lawrence, *The Practice of the Presence of God*,
H. R. Allenson, 1906, pp. 49–50)

On dark days and days when peril is near at hand, I like to light a candle to remind that I have to just turn to the light for the Light of the World is ever with me. This is to affirm I am not alone for my God is ever near: no matter how great my trouble or how dark the day, I am not left to fend for myself. If even a candle is not available I seek to affirm that I am surrounded by the love and light of God. I often say, 'The Lord is my light and my salvation.' Learn to do this throughout the day and let the words help to strengthen your relationship with God; repeat, 'The Lord is my light and my salvation.'

The Lord is

Lord, you are here, at this very moment.

Lord, you are around me and within me. He may be unseen yet he is very near.

Lord, my life and yours are woven together.

The Lord is my light no matter how dark the day.

Lord you are the light that cannot be overcome, cannot be extinguished.

Lord, you are my salvation. In you I shall not perish but have everlasting life.

Lord, you are my light and my salvation.

GOD'S AIDING

May God be aiding me,
May God be succouring me,
May God be aiding me
When near the reefs.

What Shall I Fear?

May God be safeguarding me
When among the lepers,
May God be safeguarding me
When in narrow course.

The Son of God shielding me from harm,
The Son of God shielding me from ill,
The Son of God shielding me from mishap,
The Son of God shielding me this night.

The Son of God shielding me with might,
The Son of God shielding me with power;
Each one who is dealing with me aright,
So may God deal with his soul.
(*Carmina Gadelica* III, pp. 99–101)

Some have suggested that prayers for help are a sign of weakness. I would suggest that to believe we can always cope on our own is an act of lunacy. To know that we have help at hand, far from diminishing us gives us the courage to continue and even to triumph. Life may be plain sailing for a while, the seas calm and the day bright but the chance of a storm is always there. Sometimes there are reefs that would destroy the little craft we call life. At other times the journey is through narrow straits and there is danger and trouble on every side. Suddenly we are aware that there are powers that are beyond our control and that we cannot stand in our own strength. But then we rejoice in the presence and power of the Almighty.

In what has been called the 'post-Christian' era in the West there is the great danger that we are encouraged to be self-sufficient. Such a term is untrue to life: none of us can stand alone or survive alone. We need each other and there are times when we need help that is from beyond ourselves. Much in our human make-up and in society still contains anger, violence, along with frailty and temporality. We may no longer believe in demons or evil spirits but there is no doubt there is much evil let loose upon the earth. Crime figures, acts of violence, and greed increase. There is little respect for people or property when we make self the centre of life. Powers of disintegration, destruction and divisions

65

are all let loose upon the world, as they have always been. There are times when we need a Saviour, a Redeemer. So many Celtic prayers celebrate the deliverance from fear through the protection and presence of God. The Christ is seen as the Strong One, the mighty hero triumphing over all that the powers of evil can throw against him. As the Celtic peoples often suffered persecution and being edged out of their lands and livelihood, they had a good companion in Jesus. As he was not overcome by evil but overcame evil with good, so he can come to their aid. Christ never promised an easy life for his followers, rather he warned them of rejection and even of crucifixion and death. But at the same time they were offered deliverance through the resurrection and the gift of eternal life. We are not to underestimate the powers of evil. We have to be honest and admit life is often a battle, but we have to rejoice that victory is ours through him who loves us.

It is good to look at the life of Jesus without a romantic view. See how from the start he faced opposition. He starts life in a stable and is soon a refugee. Later he was being edged out of the synagogues, out of communities; he would be edged out of the city and edged out of life. He was scorned and rejected, betrayed with a kiss, deserted by friends, misrepresented, misunderstood and left on his own without any possessions or human aid. But he did not submit to evil for evil: he did not go against the love of God. He sought to do the Father's will to the very last. But in his death he showed that in the love of God goodness will not be defeated for ever. In the end we shall overcome and rejoice in the fullness of life eternal, for we know that he who suffered on the cross is alive and is the Holy and Strong One who rescues us from death.

This reminds me of a simple scene after a school play on a dark night. I expressed concern about a little lad who would have to make a long journey in the dark. He insisted he was not afraid. How could he be afraid? But because I seemed to bother him for a while he went and found a large torch and said, 'How can I be afraid with this?'. I was delighted for him but more was to come for he then said, 'And my dad is coming for me'. Can you not see here an image of the one who delivers from darkness and brings us to life in all its fullness. In his name we can venture.

Affirm:

> Goodness is stronger than evil;
> Love is stronger than hate;
> Light is stronger than darkness;
> Life is stronger than death;
> Victory is ours through him who loves us.
> (Desmond Tutu, *An African Prayer Book*,
> Hodder and Stoughton, 1995, p. 80)

PRAYER OF DISTRESS

> May the cross of the crucifixion tree
> Upon the wounded back of Christ
> Deliver me from distress,
> From death and from spells.
>
> The cross of Christ without fault,
> All outstretched towards me;
> O God bless to me my lot
> Before my going out.
>
> What harm soever may be therein
> May I not take hence,
> For the sake of Christ the guileless,
> For the sake of the King of power.
>
> In the name of the King of life,
> In the name of the Christ of love,
> In the name of the Holy Spirit,
> The Triune of my strength.
> (*Carmina Gadelica* III, p. 73)

The cross is very evident in prayers of the Celts, for it is the greatest symbol of the love of God and of salvation. They would sign themselves with a sign of the cross as a reminder of their faith and of the signing at their baptism. To make the sign of the cross was an immediate reminder that our protection, our well-being, our survival, all depend upon God. I remember well singing at the service of Compline at Kelham College with the Society of the Sacred Mission in Lent:

> The cross does chase all evil,
> before it darkness flieth.

How often the cross has brought comfort, hope and courage to those who are troubled or distressed. In times of trouble and darkness one of the great acts of redemption is to know you are loved. We can survive far more, and fare far better if we know we are not alone and someone cares for us. I understand what St John meant when he said, 'There is no fear in love but perfect love drives out fear'. What can I fear if God is near? I am not left alone and I am loved by God. Here I would slowly learn that it is only by knowing God and his love that we can learn to love and it is only by loving we can know God. It is when God dwells in our heart we truly learn to love; and when we love we come closer and closer to God. I would know that it is in love that God triumphs over evil. His victory is not one of force but of love.

At college I would look up at the great Kelham rood which showed a very mighty figure upon the cross. This was no weakling giving in to fate but the Christ who triumphed over evil, over all that the world could throw at him. His triumph was one of light over darkness, and goodness over evil, a triumph of love. The Christ showed that all evil and powers of disintegration are powerless against love. No matter what was done to him, no matter what forces came against him, love was and is victorious. This Christ is our Redeemer. As I looked up to this heroic Christ words from the Principles of the Society of the Sacred Mission often came to mind:

> In regard to outer things, first it is necessary that you should exercise such self-mastery that there is nothing you cannot lay easily aside. You must leave all one day whether you will or not . . .

> If you have given your whole life to God, why should you prefer to lose it in this way rather than that?

If it cost you your life, what better could you ask than the time of trial be very short, since the reward is the same?

There is always a danger of misusing the sign of the cross and treating it like a charm to ward off evil or defeat. As if we were making God do something for us, as if by the cross we were demanding protection. The wearing of a cross or the signing of the cross is not protection in itself but it is a reminder of our salvation. The signing of the cross does not make God do anything; it reminds us of what God has done for us. It tells us of how deeply God loves us. It reveals how he willingly gives himself to us and for us. The difference between charms, which are in the realm of magic, and signing with the cross, which is an affirmation, is the first seeks to make something happen, the second rejoices in what God is doing and has done. Magic says 'do this' and the Christian says 'thy will be done'.

The cross is at the very heart of their understanding of the love of God, of his outpouring of himself for us and for our salvation. Monks would often pray in cross vigil, holding out their arms horizontal to the ground and praying for long lengths. I once made the mistake of saying I would do the intercessions in cross vigil at a youth event and the young folk could add their prayers. They made sure we prayed for a long time! My arms ached, tears came to my eyes, I was aware of how costly all prayer is if it is 'through Jesus Christ our Lord'.

In the Celtic lands there are remains of large stone crosses and most of these are decorated to tell a story. Many of the high crosses show Adam and Eve with an apple to depict the fallen state of humankind. Without the love and redemption of God we are unable to reach to the capacity for which we were created. The cross is essentially a symbol of the power of the love of God. There were high standing crosses in many monasteries full of geometric design. Throughout the land crosses stood as meeting places and of reminders of the love of God. Standing as they did in open countryside they spoke of God's love for the whole world and of a God not confined to church buildings or even of religion: a God who is there in our midst; reminding us of the love of God and how the Christ gave himself for the whole world.

Spend some time looking at a crucifix and seek to be aware of the love of God for you. God has given himself for you and gives himself to you in love. Accept that love; let it into your heart. Know how much God cares for you. In his eyes you are precious to him. Know that God does not seek to triumph over you or control you. As he gives himself in love, this is the response he seeks from you. You may like to use this prayer:

> On the Holy Cross I see
> Jesus' arms outstretched for me.
> Loving Jesus let me be
> Still and quiet close to thee.
> Learning all thy love for me:
> Giving all my love to thee.
>   (source unknown)

BLESSING OF A HOUSE

> Be Christ's cross on your new dwelling,
> Be Christ's cross on your new hearth,
> Be Christ's cross on your new abode,
> Upon your new fire blazing.
>
> Be Christ's cross on your topmost grain,
> Be Christ's cross on your fruitful wives,
> Be Christ's cross on your virile sons,
> Upon your conceptive daughters.
>
> Be Christ's cross on your means and portion,
> Be Christ's cross on your kin and people,
> Be Christ's cross on you each light and darkness,
> Each day and each night of your lives,
> Each day each night of your lives.
>   (*Carmina Gadelica* III, p. 367)

As a church is consecrated to God by the signing of the cross, so the Celts consecrated their home, their families and their loved ones. Not only did they sign their house, but their hearth also as it is the centre of the house. Let God be known in the centre of your home. The whole family was signed to show they belonged to God. For them the cross is a symbol of the love of God. It is a reminder that at all times and in all places God cares for them with an everlasting love. Sometimes it is good to look at a cross and repeat the words of John 3.16; or to sign oneself with the cross and simply affirm Jesus loves me. Know that you and your home are blessed by God's presence. There is a very real sense in which your home and you are as holy as any church building, for God is there with you. There is a need today to rediscover that the very ground we walk on is holy ground. We do not make God come to us. God comes with the territory. He is with us. We need to find ways of opening our eyes and our hearts to this reality. We need to have reminders of his love so that we can receive it and give our love to him.

There is nothing in life outside of God's love and care. To be signed with the cross is to declare we believe that all of life is in the hand of God and nothing is beyond his reach or care. Truly blessed is the house that knows of the love and presence of God. Today, when wearing a cross is often banned and the sign of the cross has disappeared from many schools and public places, we need to take seriously the use of this symbol as a means to teach about the saving love of God. Before Christ the cross was a symbol of human helplessness and hopelessness: it was a sign of how powerless we are against forces of evil. It was a reminder of how easy it is for the powers of disintegration, despair and destruction to triumph. Now these powers are still at work in the world and can soon overwhelm any of us. We need to be able to show that the Christ is able to rescue from greater storms than wind and waves. He is able to help us and strengthen us when the powers of darkness seem to triumph. He who was broken on the cross can bring hope to those who suffer from broken hopes and broken dreams. In Christ a breakdown is not the end but a journey to renewal and restoration. Even death is conquered by him. To be signed with the cross

71

is to show that we pass from darkness to light and in Christ life is eternal. This is something the world badly needs to know. But how will it know unless we proclaim him, and how can we proclaim him if we do not know him?

To be able to proclaim Christ we need to make him our companion and friend. We need to get to know him and his presence with us. One of the failings of the Church is we have often sent people out on mission with second-hand or book knowledge, when we should have waited until they had built up a personal relationship to their God. No amount of theological training will substitute for a personal faith. No amount of mind knowledge will compensate for not personally knowing Christ. We need to be God-filled people with our hearts overflowing with this love. This certainly seemed to be one of the great characteristics of the people of Celtic lands. They were a people that rejoiced in his love and in his saving power. They could proclaim their God by their actions because they were at home with him and he was known in their homes. This in itself is a challenge to many Christians of today who seem to have given God a religious slot but not allowed him fully into their lives or into what is happening around them.

It is good to remind yourself of the love and presence of God through the sign of the cross. This sign most of you received at your baptism to show that you belonged to God and God gives himself to you. I like to think about those I love and about my godchildren also signed in this way. Here is a prayer I sometimes say for each of them when I think in this way; make this prayer yours. It comes from the 'Signing of the Cross' in the baptism service:

> May almighty God deliver you from the powers of darkness,
> restore in you the image of his glory,
> and lead you in the light and obedience of Christ.
>
> (*Common Worship: Christian Initiation*,
> Church House Publishing, 2006, p. 68)

God to Surround Me

THE THREE

> The Three Who are over me,
> The Three Who are below me,
> The Three Who are above me here,
> The Three Who are above me yonder:
> The Three Who are in the earth,
> The Three Who are in the air,
> The Three Who are in the heaven,
> The Three Who are in the great pouring sea.
>
> > (*Carmina Gadelica* III, p. 93)

This prayer comes from a section marked 'prayers for protection': a reminder that whatever is happening to us God is with us and God Cares for us. To acknowledge the presence is not to escape from what is happening around us but to affirm we are not left abandoned to our fate. Throughout the prayers from the Hebrides there is a suggestion that though often alone these people did not suffer from the loneliness of many people who live in the cities. They were not left alone in the world for they were in the heart of God and God was in their heart.

Faith in the Holy Trinity is not an assent to a dogma, or simply saying 'I believe'. The Scriptures tell us that even the devil believes. Faith is a renewing of our relationship with God in every new situation and event. Faith is a commitment of love to a loving God who is ever with us and never leaves us. This prayer, this commitment is not a burden imposed upon us or a duty, it is a source of knowing we are loved and so becomes a source of power and lightness.

There is hardly another nation, apart from the Jews, that has so many prayers by lay people about the presence of God. This prayer in fact reflects much of what is said in Psalm 139.5–10:

75

> You hem me in, behind and before and lay your hand upon me.
> Such knowledge is too wonderful for me; it is so high that I
>   cannot attain it.
> Where can I go from your spirit? Or where can I flee from your
>   presence?
> If I ascend to heaven you are there; if I make my bed in Sheol,
>   you are there.
> If I take the wings of the morning and settle in the farthest
>   limits of the sea,
> even there your hand shall lead me, and your right hand hold
>   me fast.

Spend some time rejoicing in this reality; above all do not project God's presence to another place or time. This is the God who is: the Father, Son and Holy Spirit are with us. You may like to begin by saying, 'I am in the presence, the power and the peace of Father, Son and Holy Spirit.' Be still and let these words be known as a reality. God the creator of all there is, your creator, is with you. Take time to talk to him and give thanks for his creation. Rejoice that he made you and that you are his.

Christ is alive and not just a figure of history; the risen Lord is with you. He is your Saviour. He came down that you may be raised up. He comes and offers his presence and peace to you. Learn to walk with him and know he walks with you, and accept his gift of peace. Seek to discover his presence in your work and in your relaxation. Get to know him as your Redeemer.

The Holy Spirit, the Lord and giver of Life, is with you to inspire and strengthen you. The very power of God is being offered to you as the Spirit gives himself to you. Know that the very breath of life is a gift from God. Not only does he give life, he restores and refreshes you. This is the presence in which you live. Now say:

> The Three Who are over me.

Yes they ARE, so do not be put off. They are with you to encourage, to guide and strengthen you. They are over you like a shield to protect you and keep you in life eternal.

> The Three Who are below me.

What a wonderful thought: even in the depths God is with us. No matter how far we fall, no matter how deep we plunge. Our God can be met and is there to uphold us and make sure we do not perish.

The Three Who are above me here.

Wherever you are God is above you. He is the God who seeks to raise you, to lift you into the fullness of eternal life. He may be beyond your sight and your knowledge but he is not beyond you or your heart. Learn to ascend to him now in heart and mind.

The Three Who are above me yonder.

You may not know what lies ahead but know *who* is there. You are not alone, for you are enfolded in the love of the Holy Three. If you project years ahead you may fear where you may be – why fear when you know who is with you. Nothing can separate you from the love of God.

Rejoice that as God is with you; he has not left his world. The presence of God is woven into the very fabric of all that there is. Though nothing can fully contain God, God can be found in all his fullness in all things:

> The Three Who are in the earth,
> The Three Who are in the air,
> The Three Who are in the heaven,
> The Three Who are in the great pouring sea.

Wherever you are God is with you. God uses his creation to speak to us. Matter is not separate from God, though God cannot be confused with it or fully contained in it. Do not divide into sacred and secular, for all comes from God and belongs to him. Affirm through the day:

> You, Lord, are in this place,
> your presence fills it,
> your presence is peace.

THE ENCIRCLING OF CHRIST

> Christ as a light,
> Illumine and guide me!
> Christ as a shield o'ershadow and cover me!
> Christ be under me! Christ be over me!
> Christ be beside me,
> On left hand and right!
> Christ be before me, behind me, about me!
> Christ this day, be within and without me!

This part of James Clarence Mangan's translation of 'St Patrick's Breastplate' first appeared in *Duffy's Magazine* and was later printed in Mangan's *Collected Poems* (New York, 1859). A more familiar translation of the hymn is Mrs Alexander's 'I Bind unto Myself Today', which was sung at York Minster on St Patrick's Day in 1891 when Archbishop Magee, an Irishman, was enthroned. Sadly this hymn is now missing from many of our hymnbooks.

I have taught this prayer to school and pilgrim groups visiting Holy Island. I called it 'The Prayer of Seven Directions'. I prefer to give it a more flowing movement, making an encircling prayer of it: Christ before me, on my right, behind me, on my left, beneath me, above me – and within me. I encouraged young people and adults to act it out as we faced each direction in turn. I made sure they understood; they were not making Christ come, rather they were opening their lives to Christ who ever comes to them, who is always with them. The prayer is our coming to him and calling upon his love and his aid. Again, this is not positive thinking; it is far more, for it is tuning in to a reality, the fact that Christ is with us.

We began by facing the East, the place of the rising sun, the start of the day.

> Christ before me.

At the beginning of life, at the beginning of each minute, at the beginning of any new event, wherever we go, whatever we do, Christ is waiting to meet us. We may not know what lies ahead, but we know who waits for us. Start each day by seeking to meet Christ who comes to meet you. Give your self in love who gives himself to you.

Christ on my right.

Turning to the south, the direction of the midday sun. Christ is there in the thick of life. Christ in our work and activity. Christ present in the fullness of life, in our dexterity and our abilities at the peak of all that we do. Christ is with us in all we seek to do or achieve. In him we find strength and courage.

Christ behind me.

Turning west to where the sun goes down. Christ is there behind us to protect us against our own past. He is there when power fails and we discover our frailty. He comes with forgiveness and seeks to give us rest and peace. He is there to protect us from anything that would sneak up upon us to hurt us. He is with us on the sunset road, often unnoticed but always there. When powers wane and the lights go dim he is still there. Though we cannot see him he is still with us.

Christ on my left.

We now face the darkness of the north where the sun does not reach. Christ is present in our darkness and in the darkness of the world. When sinister things are happening to us and in the world around us, Christ never leaves us. It is often at this moment we know we need a power and a light that is not of our making. It is when we face darkness within or without we know we need a Saviour. We need him who is the Light of the World. In his strength alone we can face that last great darkness of death.

Christ beneath me.

At this point we can touch the earth. We need to remember we are of the dust of the earth and only in the Love of God can we hope for life eternal. This is the Christ who descended, who went into the depths of life, who descended into all the hells of this world and even into death. He is there to uphold. 'Underneath are the everlasting arms.' However deep we sink we will find that he is there. In times of trouble let his strength bear you up. If you look at the hands that bear you up they are hands of love that bear the imprint of the nails of the cross.

Christ above me.

Stretch up high. Know that though God is higher than your thoughts he can be reached by love. Stretch out and reach for the love of God. Christ, who descended to the earth, also ascended into heaven. He came down with a purpose, to lift us up. He died that we might live. He entered the grave that we might rise to eternal life. He became human that we might share in the Divine. Lift up your hearts and rejoice.

We have now completed six directions. This can be expressed in the words, 'We are in the heart of God: we are encircled by God', or we can affirm, 'In him we live and move and have our being' (Acts 17.28). Once we express that God is greater than we are and that we cannot fully contain him, we can now say:

Christ within me.

I like children to point at themselves as they say these words, and to acknowledge that Christ is in each of us. Like the air we breathe, God is all around us and within us. We do not need to travel to find the Christ, for he is with us and about us. Be still and know that the Lord is here: his Spirit is with us. We are called to see Christ in others, and to be Christ to others. Let Christ work within us. Let us respect the Christ in others. We would turn to someone near us and say, 'the Lord is with you' and they would reply, 'also with you'. Rejoice in this reality.

ENCOMPASSING

The compassing of God be on thee,
The compassing of the God of life.

The compassing of Christ be on thee,
The compassing of the Christ of love.

The compassing of the Spirit be on thee,
The compassing of the Spirit of Grace.

The compassing of the Three be on thee,
The compassing of the Three preserve thee,
The compassing of the Three preserve thee.
(*Carmina Gadelica* III, p. 105)

The encompassing prayers or encircling prayers are variations of the prayer of seven directions. Their aim is the same: to declare that we are immersed in the presence and love of God, that we are surrounded by him and enfolded in his love. Making such an affirmation is said to be making a Caim. Very often to make the caim you would face east and raise your right hand and point forwards. Then you would turn slowly in a sun-wise or clockwise direction until you had completed a circle. While you are doing this you can simply say, 'Circle me, O God' or 'God Encompass me' or 'God is about me'. The Celts chose to go sun-wise and it was called 'going deasil'; the opposite to this is widdershins which was going against the clock and the way of the world. The Celts warned if you went against the way of the world too often, something terrible was likely to happen to you. This in itself is acting out a truth: we cannot be seeking help from God if we are going against nature. I can remember in an early woodwork class I took a plane apart about three times and sharpened the blade. The lesson was nearly over when the teacher came and said, 'It is no use sharpening the blade if you will continue to go against the grain!' There is a lesson for life. If you go against the grain in nature you should expect life to be rough.

The encompassing prayer is a retuning of our lives to the reality of the love and power of God. In your room at this very minute radio waves fill the air and even pass through you. But if you do not switch on a receiver and tune to a station you will not receive what is being offered to you. Your radio does not create the programme. It is available to you, it is there, if you tune in to it. In the same way the Caim is a way of tuning in to the protecting love of God that is ever available.

When Celtic saints met trouble or evil they would draw the Caim around themselves as a person would pull a cloak around them in a storm. Because we are not almighty it is not an excuse for opting out, for running away, or for wallowing in our troubles. Though we cannot lift ourselves by our own shoestrings and though there are times when we cannot pull ourselves together, help is at hand. We need to acknowledge our help comes from the Lord who made heaven and earth. There are times when we exhaust ourselves by going on alone when we should rest and acknowledge the need of help. There are certainly times when we are not able to rise under our own steam. There is need to know there is a 'very present help in trouble', and put our faith in God. Rather than weaken us this gives us the courage to stand and to withstand, for we are not in our strength alone. There is something wonderful about being able to sing:

> In heav'nly love abiding,
> no change my heart shall fear;
> and safe is such confiding, for nothing changes here:
> the storm may roar without me,
> my heart may low be laid;
> but God is round about me
> and can I be dismayed?
>
> (Anna Laetitia Waring, 1820–1910)

It must be remembered that this heavenly love is not about some-one who has left this earth but about someone who is rejoicing in the love and power of God now while struggling with the ways of the world. Learn to practise the Caim until you can personally say with some assurance, 'We dwell in him and he in us.' Acknowledge God is all around you and say,

> Circle me, O God
> Keep hope within
> Despair without.
>
> Circle me, O God,
> Keep peace within
> Keep turmoil out.

Circle me, O God,
Keep calm within
Keep storms without.

Circle me, O God,
Keep strength within
Keep weakness out.
(David Adam, *The Edge of Glory*,
    Triangle/SPCK, 1985, p. 8)

JESUS THE ENCOMPASSER

My Christ! my Christ! my shield my encircler,
Each day, each night, each light, each dark;
My Christ! my Christ! my shield my encircler,
Each day, each night, each light, each dark.

Be near me to uphold me, my treasure, my triumph,
In my lying, in my standing, in my watching, in my sleeping.

Jesus, Son of Mary! my helper, my encircler,
Jesus, Son of David! my strength everlasting;
Jesus, Son of Mary! my helper, my encircler,
Jesus, Son of David! my strength everlasting;
                    (*Carmina Gadelica* III, p. 77)

I can remember once going on a walk across a moor in
Northumberland and being anxious about making sure I read the
map properly. Twice I had to retrace my steps, for I had wandered
off the way and once ended up in a boggy area I should have
avoided. When I went back home I told a friend of this venture
and he replied, 'I wish you had told me. It is one of my favourite
walks. I could have gone with you and showed you the way. You
should have called.' I wonder how often we get lost, feel lonely or

get into trouble simply because we do not call for help. We are too willing to go in our own strength alone. Human pride or sheer ignorance makes us strive on our own. How often help is at hand and we do not accept it. Christ would walk the road with us and be our companion if only we would call upon him. When we need a shield against harm or against temptation we should learn to call upon Jesus and let him be a strength to us. He would gladly walk the road with us as he walked the road to Emmaus with those who had lost hope (see Luke 24.13–35). Quite often we have failed to get help which is at hand by not asking for it. We need to invite Jesus to abide with us, for he will not force himself upon us.

I am a fan of science fiction and like programmes such as *Star Trek*. It would seem wherever the human being goes in the whole universe there are always dangers and alien forces at hand. There are powers that are ready to invade our lives and destroy us. There is no place in the universe that is free from forces of evil and of destruction. There is always a battle between good and evil, between light and darkness. There are times when the human being seems so fragile and could easily be diminished. I go along with this, for it is often the experience of life. At such times the members of the space craft would raise around their vessel a force field. This is a shield from harm and a protection in the battle. The force field was available; it was there, if only they had the sense to use it. Is not this an image of our journey through the universe? We are not able to live without also facing harm, mishap or ill. No matter how clever we are or strong we are, we cannot travel on for ever in our own strength. There are always forces that are mightier than we are. But we are never left alone. The power of the Almighty comes to our aid. Christ is ready to rescue and redeem us. He will be our guide and companion on the journey. But many of us are like the disciples in the storm, we travel with 'Jesus asleep' in the boat. We have never awakened him by calling upon him. We often travel alone and in our own power, and the danger is that such power is limited. Learn to call him by name; invite him to be your friend and your companion in your travels and in your life. Take time each day to allow him into your life and to share with you. You may like to use this prayer:

Christ, come! Come to me! Come to my aid.
Let your presence be all around me
In your presence is peace.

Christ, come! Come to me! Come to my home.
Let your presence be all around me
In your presence is love.

Christ, come! Come to me! Come to my home.
Let your presence be all around me
In your presence is strength.

GOD'S AID

God to enfold me,
God to surround me,
God in my speaking,
God in my thinking.

God in my sleeping,
God in my waking,
God in my watching,
God in my hoping.

God in my life,
God in my lips,
God in my soul,
God in my heart.

God in my sufficing,
God in my slumber,
God in mine ever-living soul,
God in mine eternity.
  (*Carmina Gadelica* III, p. 53)

There is a danger that the centre of many prayers is not God but
ourselves and our own needs. We come with a shopping list of

demands when we ought to be seeking to know God's love and his will for us. We come to give God directions and requests when we should be enjoying his presence and abiding in him. Before all prayer we should seek to know we are enfolded in the love of God. We should learn to rest in, and rejoice in, his presence and his love. For this reason I have taught for a long time, if you feel you have only five minutes for prayer, spend four of those minutes just knowing that God is all about you and loves you.

One of my favourite images of the love of God is the return of the Prodigal Son. You may like to read the story in Luke 15.11–32. After leaving the presence and protection of his father and going into a far country where he hungered and felt alone, the prodigal decides to return to the father. He will confess his sin and offer to be a slave. As he turns and makes for home he discovers the father runs to meet him. Running is hardly a seemly thing for an eastern man to do, yet the father hastens to meet him. The father has been waiting for this day. He would not force his son to return but he has been waiting for him. All of the time, his heart has been going out toward his son in love. The father had been waiting for this return. The son is not accepted back on any terms but love. He is accepted back not as a slave but as a son. The father enfolds him in his arms and surrounds him with his love. This moment of being wrapped in a warm embrace is the beginning of his homecoming. In the same way we can come home to God and allow him to enfold us in his love.

Do you let God enfold you in his love each day? Have you learned to abide in that love and to rejoice in that love? Take to heart the words of Julian of Norwich: 'He is our clothing. In his love he wraps and holds us. He enfolds us for love, and he will never let us go.' (Julian of Norwich, *Enfolded in Love*, Darton, Longman and Todd, 1980, p. 1)

And again:

> As the body is clad in clothes, and the flesh in skin, and the bones in flesh, and the heart in the whole, so are we clothed, body and soul, in the goodness of God and enfolded in it.
>
> (Julian of Norwich, *Enfolded in Love*, p. 6)

God to Surround Me

Begin where all things have their beginning, God.
God, who created you and who created all things is with you
God loves you and every single cell of your body.
God enfolds you and wraps you around with his presence.
Rest in him and rejoice in him.
Now seek to know this great all surrounding God is in your
    heart
God in your life: God in your ever living soul.
Open your mind to that reality that God is within you and
    about you
God is with you.

Here is a well known prayer often used in Communion; let it express your communion at this very moment with God:

God be in my head, and in my understanding;
God be in my eyes, and in my looking;
God be in my mouth, and in my speaking;
God be in my heart and in my thinking;
God be at my end, and at my departing.
                (from Pynson's *Horae*, 1514)

Think often upon these words of Hilary of Poitiers from his 'Treatise on the Trinity':

I came to see that there is no space without God: space does not
exist apart from God. God is in heaven, in hell and beyond the seas.
God lives in everything and enfolds everything. God embraces all
that is, and is embraced by the universe: confined to no part within it he encompasses all that exists.
    (Robert Atwell, *Celebrating the Saints*, SCM Press, 2004, p. 37)

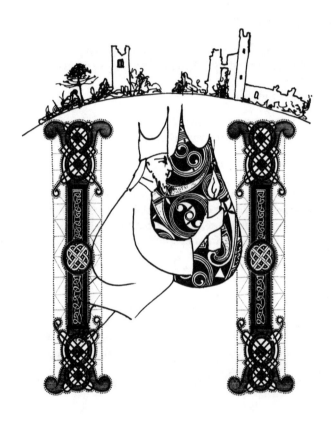

The Power of God

BLESSINGS

The eye of the great God be upon you,
The eye of the God of glory be on you,
The eye of the Son of Mary Virgin be on you,
The eye of the Spirit mild be on you,
To aid you and to shepherd you;
Oh the kindly eye of the Three be on you,
To aid you and to shepherd you.

(Carmina Gadelica III, p. 201)

The Celtic people were forever offering blessings to each other and calling upon God to use his power to bless them, their homes, their flocks, their work, their rest. There was nothing that was seen to be outside the power or the blessing of God. They were aware that God sought to pour his love and his blessing upon all creation. It is often only our own hardness, or preoccupation, that does not allow the blessing of God to take place. God is with us waiting for us to call upon him, for us to open our life to him, so that he can bless us and give himself to us. To invoke a blessing is to call upon and open our life to the power of God.

Blessings are what God bestows upon us, continually. His whole action towards us is blessing, from the blessing of life itself to the gifts he showers upon us. The greatest blessings are the gift of himself, and the gift of eternal life. No blessing is ours by right, but in his love he offers them to us all freely. What we are asked to do is to respond, to allow the blessing to work, and to see the love and power of God at work in our lives.

Blessings must not be confined to a church service; these are only expressions of the reality of what God is doing all of the time to his creation. Blessings are to be discovered, voiced and lived in our day-to-day life. Blessings are not the domain of the priest alone even though liturgical blessings may be designed for the priest. In some circles it is said that if a lay person offers a blessing it must be preceded by the word 'may', as if their calling for a blessing was more doubtful than a priest's. There is great danger here, for blessings are not controlled by the hierarchy or by the Church. Blessings are given by God to those who call upon him. Blessings are what a mother bestows upon her family, what a worker bestows on his firm, what a good citizen bestows upon her community. And all these blessings are gifts from God to us and working through us.

When we say 'May God bless you', this is not an expression of God deciding to bless us or not. God is ever ready to give himself to us. If the 'may' expresses a possibility of not receiving a blessing this is not due to God withholding but rather to us not being open to God. God can only bless us if we allow him to enter into our life and our situation.

I believe it is good to carry blessings around with us. Even if we cannot say them out loud we can express them, visualize them and try to live them. As Christians we need to know that God is at work in the world and is ever ready to give of himself. Very often on visiting a house it is good to call for a blessing of peace upon it, even though we may not be able to say it out aloud. The Celtic Christians often did this. Here is one of their prayers that you could well learn and use:

> The peace of God be to you,
> The peace of Christ be to you,
> The peace of the Spirit be to you,
> And to your children,
> To you and your children.
> (*Carmina Gadelica* III, p. 201)

In this prayer, as with all blessings, God is the subject and active. It is his blessing and we are the instrument. God bestows his blessings to us and through us. If we are aware that we are living in the peace and love of God, that peace will then flow out from us to others. Though it must also be said that if we are not at peace with those around us, then through our own fault we cannot be living in the peace of God. The blessings that God gives are not given to be hoarded but to be shared with all around us. It is by sharing what we have received that we make room for God to pour more in.

Very often I have discovered that if I have sought to give a blessing – even non-verbal – I have more often received a blessing in turn. In seeking to share blessings we discover that they are not a one-way process: the giver often receives, the God whom we seek to bring meets us there. The person we sought to help is often a great help to us. With God's blessings the traffic as always is three-way: flowing to us from God, from us to others and from others to us. The traffic is also between heaven and earth, and earth and heaven. Once this way is open, we begin to discover life in all its fullness.

Learn to share blessings with others all the time. Let 'the peace of God be with you', 'the love of God fill you'. Prayers spoken out loud or thought during the day will help us to know that our God, his peace and his blessings are open to us and are at work in the world. Blessings affirm God is at work in the world and is with us. Here is a blessing you could learn and use for your life and your home:

> The LORD bless you and keep you;
> the LORD make his face to shine upon you, and be gracious
>   to you;
> the LORD lift up his countenance upon you, and give you
>   peace.

(Numbers 6.24–26)

THE POWER OF GOD

> I summon today all these powers between me and those evils,
> Against every cruel merciless power that may oppose my body
>   and soul,
> Against incantations and false prophets,
> Against black laws of pagandom,
> Against false laws of heretics,

Against craft of idolatry,
Against spells of women and smiths and wizards,
Against every knowledge that corrupts man's body and soul.
(St Patrick, *c.* 385–461)

From the Tripartite *Life of St Patrick* (edited Whitley Stokes, 1877, Vol I, p. 41), we are given the information of Patrick's coming to Tara: 'They left their vessel in the estuary and went along the land until they came to Ferta Fer Fiacc (the graves of Fiacc's men) and Patrick's tent was pitched in that place, and he struck the Paschal fire'. So Patrick not only announced his presence but his intention. He is there to declare the Christian faith and the power of the risen Lord. The Easter festival coincided with the great pagan festival at Tara when all lights were to be extinguished and all fires put out to show the king was in control. Only the king could provide light and fire and only from him could it be received. Patrick challenged this and so was challenging the king. The Paschal fire blazed out and lit up the whole of Mag Breg. The king's wise men warned him unless this fire was extinguished it would flood all of Ireland with light and burn until Doomsday. The Prayer we know as 'St Patrick's Breastplate' or as the 'Deer's Cry' is linked with this occasion. The prayer may be only attributed to St Patrick and could belong to three centuries later. But there is a sense in which that does not matter, for this prayer expresses so well the early Celtic Christian faith and the power of the risen Lord. Here is celebrated the triumph of light over darkness, and the risen Lord over death. It is in the power of God we are able to arise and in his power alone. No one but God can offer us the light of eternal life. Look how in Kuno Meyer's translation of 'The Deer's Cry' Patrick continually attributes to God his ability to arise:

I arise today
Through a mighty strength, the invocation of the Trinity . . .
I arise today
Through the strength of Christ's birth with his baptism,
Through the strength of his crucifixion with his burial
Through the strength of resurrection with his ascension,
Through the strength of his descent for the judgement of Doom.

I arise today
Through the strength of the love of the Cherubim . . .
I arise today
Through the strength of heaven . . .

I arise today
Through God's strength to pilot me.

All of this precedes the quotation at the beginning of this section. It is through this strength of God Patrick can stand against the powers of evil and opposition. He believed and trusted in God's power to save and in the power of Christ we will triumph. Patrick knew he was involved in a battle and he would need to call upon all the powers of God if he were to survive. Elsewhere he tells of how easily he could die and how often his life has been in danger. He has no illusion that he is free from death. But there is a sense in which he is free from defeat for he believed 'victory is ours through him who loves us' (see Romans 8.35–39).

Yet we must understand what kind of victory this is. The crucifixion shows us what can often happen to good people. It reveals there is no real justice in this world, for the evil often triumph and the good suffer. God does not seek to triumph over people by force but only by love. God is not taking up arms against evil, not defeating it with his might – that is not his way. God chooses the terms on which he will fight and his weapon is love. No one will be forced to obey, no one forced to accept, no one made to enter the kingdom. They will be invited and the invitation is one of love. Of course, it follows that if we excuse ourselves we exclude ourselves from God and from his kingdom.

God in Christ defeats darkness and evil by rejecting their terms by offering himself in love. It has often been said, it was not the nails that kept Christ on the cross but love. The Paschal fire is a symbol of light triumphing over darkness and love triumphing over hate. Patrick would enter Tara without a battle and from here the light of Christ would spread. Patrick entered in the power of God and that power is the power of love. This love does not stand by and let evil triumph. The cross is not about a God who allows goodness to be defeated: it is a God who triumphs through love. Love is light-giving and life-giving.

Will we allow that love to work in our lives and through us to others? We come not to possess but to give ourselves as Christ gave himself for us: to reveal the love of God in all our actions and relationships. This is only possible when we know we are loved, that God loves us and in that love protects us. We rejoice that nothing can separate us from the love of God in Christ Jesus.

Read again Romans 8.35–39 and give thanks for that love. Affirm that you arise today in that love using the affirmations from 'The Deer's Cry' printed above.

GRACE

> Thanks to Thee, God,
> Who brought'st me from yesterday
> To the beginning of today,
> Everlasting joy
> To earn for my soul
> With good intent.
> And for every gift of peace
> Thou bestowest on me,
> My thoughts, my words,
> My deeds, my desires
> I dedicate to Thee,
> I supplicate Thee,
> I beseech Thee,
> To keep me from offence,
> And to shield me to-night,
> For the sake of Thy wounds,
> With Thine offering of grace.
> (*Carmina Gadelica* I, p. 99)

All of creation is dependent on God's continuing grace. Each day we arise by the grace of God and in God's grace. If God were to withdraw his grace nothing would exist. It is by his grace all things have their being. Grace is the power and the presence of God ever present and working through his out-going love. Grace is God's covenanted relationship with human kind and is seen in his relationship with Israel. This grace is revealed in its fullest in our Lord Jesus Christ for here the outpouring of God's redeeming love is revealed in his giving of himself for the salvation of the world. Without grace there is no salvation story, there would be no Good News, no gospel to tell. Place yourself in this grace each morning by rejoicing in God's love and acknowledging he is present with you and within the world. We are not called out of the world but we are to see the world with new eyes and approach it with a new heart. The grace of God can be found and accepted in any time, in any place, in anything and in any person, if only we would look long enough and deep enough. This is not an intellectual exercise as much as one of love. It is seeing with 'the eyes of the heart'. Our lives are transformed when we know God is waiting to give himself to us, and for us to give ourselves to him. Grace tells us the kingdom of God is not far off; it is near at hand and waiting for us to enter into it (Mark 1.15).

Grace is for free. It is the free gift of God giving himself to us and for us. Grace is not dependent upon us except that we do have to be open to it. We need to learn that we cannot earn grace, we cannot deserve grace, we cannot achieve grace; it is a free gift (see Romans 11.6, Ephesians 2.4–10). Though like many gifts, grace needs to be unwrapped to be enjoyed. The grace of God is given for us to use and to allow grace to work in our lives is to have the wisdom as well as the courage to accept that we are not self-sufficient. The truth is in many situations, 'we have no power of ourselves to help ourselves'. Our help comes from the Lord who made heaven and earth. The knowledge that we are not almighty should stop us taking ourselves too seriously: grace offers us a lightness and a freedom from being over-burdened. A good way to beginning the day is to affirm:

I arise today in the power of God
I am given God's grace: the gift of his presence.
I dwell in his peace.

Sacraments are about the hidden grace of God and cannot be fully explained. Sacraments seek to bring before us the unseen love and presence of God. Sacraments are meant to speak for themselves. They are designed to bring us before the Great Other, the mystery of the God unseen yet ever near. Words cannot explain what happens in this encounter for it is living and ever changing; this relationship cannot be caged in a formula, or enclosed on a page. But it can be experienced, enjoyed and celebrated. The presence of God, hope, healing, wholeness and holiness are all gifts offered to us. A ballerina who was asked what a particular dance meant replied, 'If I could have said it, I would not have the need to dance it'. Sacraments can say more than a thousand words, as can a hug or a kiss.

The Sacrament of Communion is a celebration that we dwell in him and he in us. It is an affirmation of a truth that we have to make our own. We are people of God's grace; this means we are all gifted people, charismatic people, for God gives himself to us all. When God comes to us so do his gifts of love, joy and peace. Often we feel too busy to let his gifts get to work in our hearts and lives! The danger is we are forever giving the impression we have to work for these gifts. Within the Church and the world at large what we need to see are charismatic people at work among us more than just academics. We need to see the gifted rather than the grafted: people who are able to pour out from their store of love rather than those forever seeking to gain more by work or study. The gospel is not about book learning as much as about accepting the gift of God's redeeming love. Though, like the Celtic peoples, I am not a dualist. It is not a question of either/or, for our charismatic people need to bring their minds to bear on their gifts and our academics need to discover it is not all about work or the intellect. Learn to give thanks for the gifts God has given to you and open your life to his grace.

Lord God, come, fill us with your grace;
Surround us with your love;
Keep us aware of your presence.
Help us to give ourselves this day to you.

SERENITY

I am serene because I know Thou lovest me.
Because Thou lovest me, naught can move me from Thy peace.
Because Thou lovest me, I am as one to whom all good has
    come.
(Alistair Maclean, *Hebridean Altars*, Hodder & Stoughton, p. 73)

Life has many storms and it is not easy to remain calm or at peace. This is because what most of us call peace is dependant on circumstances and on our own ability to cope. Our security and well-being are based on many things. We seek safety in having enough possessions and insuring what we have. We feel we can only be at peace if we have financial security, otherwise our life would be too full of worry. We desire to always be in good health and to be able to fend for ourselves. We like to feel we are in control. None of these desires are bad in themselves but if our peace is totally based on them it will fail. When circumstances change, as they will, it is so easy to feel overwhelmed or storm-tossed. No one who is living life to the full will escape from such times of trouble or change. If we are sensitive we will realize we are often surrounded by threats of storms and impending disasters. For this reason I often pray:

Calm me, O Lord, as you stilled the storm
Still me, O Lord, keep me from harm.
Let all the tumult within me cease:
Enfold me, Lord, in your peace.
(David Adam, *The Edge of Glory*, Triangle/SPCK, 1985, p. 7)

This is to remind me of the presence, the power and the peace of God, that God in his love enfolds me. Of course it is necessary to allow the love of God to be at work in your life, to let it happen. It is no use seeking peace and then going out to rush from one thing to another in a restless state of mind. We must learn to rest in him and to let him be our peace.

In the study of children who have been deprived of loving attention at an early age, it was found that they were more easily upset in later life and soon made to feel insecure. Their past experience of life often reverberated in the present: their peace was often threatened because they felt they were left on their own and they did not have the power to survive on their own. This in its turn often prevented them from achieving and often made them restless. Restlessness is a sign we are not at home or at peace in the present. This prevents us from enjoying the present moment.

Restlessness and hyperactivity are not only signs of the age we live in but are also found in many churches. Too many church services are forever on the move and lack stillness. We need to learn again: 'Be still and know that I am God.' We need to make space in our lives to get to know God and his love. Activity in itself is not a bad thing. In fact as long as we are alive we need to remain active: we need to be able to move, to change, to react. But a state of 'restlessness' can be a danger to us all, for it does not allow us to be still or to rest. This in the end is life-draining and the cause of not being at ease in the present or with what is around us, which is disease. In our restlessness there seems to be heartache, a longing, for something other, and we rarely remain satisfied for long. We are not at peace with ourselves and so cannot be at peace with the world around us. The Germans have a word for this restlessness, this feeling of emptiness, and they call it 'angst'. Angst is far more than anxiety; it is a feeling of not being quite at home in the world, a feeling of being dissatisfied, a feeling of emptiness. Angst is energy-stealing and a cause of depression; it affects our whole being, for it is a trouble of the heart. Angst often arises when we feel unloved or alone.

Biblical writers used the word 'heart' more than 900 times. There is a sense that it has no precise meaning, perhaps purposely as it is describing the very centre of our being. Sometimes heart is used to describe the will, at other times the emotions, the soul, the personality or our whole being. Whatever, the biblical writers were in no doubt that the heart is made by God for God, and without God the heart is not at ease. The heart is made to contain God and nothing else will satisfy it, for it is made for the eternal. It is said there is a hole in the heart of everyone and it is a hole that only God can fill. Angst can only find a true cure when the heart is God-filled. St Augustine, who experienced this deep longing for God, emphasized this when he said: 'Lord, our hearts are restless till they rest in thee.'

Once we allow God into our hearts, into our innermost being, all of life is transformed. The division between sacred and secular, between heaven and earth begins to blur and we realize that heaven and earth are one in God. Now we can rejoice in our own being and in the place where we are, for God is with us. In resting in this love we become aware of a new harmony within all of creation, for all is in God and his love. Nothing separates us from God, not even the storms of death. Though we may lose many battles, though we may often be hard-pressed, we know that in the end victory is ours through him who loves us. What joy! What peace! Here is a prayer I use often and especially in difficult times:

> Lord, I am enfolded by you,
> Surrounded by you,
> Held closely to you.
>
> You Lord are in my heart
> Your presence fills it
> Your presence is peace.
>
> You Lord are in my heart
> Your presence fills it
> Your presence is love
> You Lord are in my heart
> Your presence fills it
> Your presence is joy.

THE BALANCED LIFE

> That I might bless the Lord
> Who orders all;
> Heaven with all its countless bright orders,
> Land strand and flood,
> That I might search in all the books
> That would help my soul;
> At times kneeling to Heaven of my heart,
> At times singing psalms;
> At times contemplating the King of Heaven,
> Chief of the Holy Ones;
> At times at work without compulsion,
> This would be delightful.
> At times picking duilisc from the rocks
> At other times fishing
> At times distributing food to the poor
> At times in a hermitage.
> (Eleanor Hull (ed.), *The Poem Book of the Gael*,
> tr. Kuno Meyer, Chatto & Windus, 1913, p. 112)

This prayer, from an Irish manuscript in the Burgundian Library in Brussels, is attributed to St Columba. It is easy to imagine saints living totally different lives from ours and spending their whole time in church and verbal prayer. Many prayers of the Celtic saints show how this is not so. Their prayers arise out of their work or their situation; they are not always in church. They do not need to be, for they know that God is present in all of life and does not need us to go to a church to be in contact with him. Columba's prayer lays out what is seen as an ideal way of living. It reveals a balanced life of prayer, study, manual work and relaxation. To be able to work without being forced to 'would be delightful'. Columba looked forward to being on the seashore and picking duilisc, an edible seaweed, from the rocks. He also hopes to go fishing. He sees himself giving out what he has received to the poor. He seeks times when he would like to be alone with nothing to disturb him so that he can turn to God. In this prayer there is no separation into sacred and secular. Everything is sacred; all that is done is within God's kingdom. God can be found in each action, in the picking of seaweed as well as in the singing of psalms. God is present when fishing or when doling out food to the poor, as well as when spending times alone with him. God does not demand one activity rather than another but rather that we find God in all of life. It is only when we find God in all that we do that life has a proper balance and harmony.

When at College I discovered that all things could be done to the glory of God. But I learnt the hard way. I was told every task could be for God's glory and that meant it had to be done well. I was then told to go and clean the urinals and 'it means cleaning where no one sees around the bends. Know that whatever you do in this world it is for the forwarding or the hindrance of God's kingdom.' I discovered that life in College was not only study and worship, it was scrubbing floors, shovelling coke, doing electrical repairs, feeding pigs and all of this was our living in God's kingdom. True, the visits to the chapel served as a constant reminder of the call of God but the manual work often helped to earth both the worship and the study, and the worship gave an added glory to all our actions. Each balanced the other.

Think on these words by Gerard Manley Hopkins about how to begin to give glory to God.

> Turn then, brethren, now and give God glory. You do say grace at meals and thank and praise God for your daily bread, so far so good, but thank and praise him now for everything. When a man is in God's grace and free from mortal sin, then everything that he does, so long as there is no sin in it, gives God glory and what does not give him glory has some, however little, sin in it. It is not only prayer that gives God glory but work. Smiting on an anvil, sawing a beam, whitewashing a wall, driving horses, sweeping, scouring, everything gives God some glory if being in his grace you do it as your duty. To go to communion worthily gives God great glory, but to take food in thankfulness and temperance gives him glory too. To lift up the hands in prayer gives God glory, but a man with a dung fork in his hand, a woman with a slop pail, give him glory too. He is so great that all things give him glory if you mean they should. So then, my brethren, live.
>
> (Gardner, W. H. (ed.), *Gerard Manley Hopkins*,
> Penguin, 1953, p. 144)

Seek to discover ways in which all of your life can give glory to God. Learn that the place on which you stand is holy ground. Say with Jacob, 'Surely the Lord is in this place, and I knew it not'. Affirm God's presence in your work place, in the regular, the common and ordinary actions of your life. Learn that God awaits you at every moment, in your leisure and rest, in your study, in your work, as well as in your worship. Remember the Lord's Prayer says: 'your kingdom come, your will be done, on earth as in heaven'. Take time to consider this which I wrote while on Lindisfarne:

> Within each piece of creation,
> within each person,
> the hidden God waits
> to surprise us with his glory.
>
> Within each moment of time,
> within each day and hour,
> the hidden God approaches us
> calling our name to make us his own.
>
> Within each human heart,
> within our innermost being,
> the hidden God touches us,
> to awaken us and to reveal his love.
>
> Everything, everyone is within God,
> all space, all time and every person.
> The hidden God asks us to open
> our eyes and our hearts to his presence.

The Borderlands

SEEING BEYOND

Be thou my vision, O Lord of my heart,
Be all else but naught to me save that thou art,
Be thou my best thought in the day and the night,
Both waking and sleeping thy presence my light.

Be thou my wisdom, be thou my true word,
Be thou ever with me, and I with thee, Lord;
Be thou my great Father, and I thy true son;
Be thou in me dwelling, and I with thee one.
(eighth-century Irish prayer, tr. Mary Byrne, 1880–1931,
and versified by Eleanor Hull, 1860–1935)

When I look at the title of some of my books I realize how I
have always been interested in borderlands. My very first book
was called *The Edge of Glory*. I have also written *Walking the Edges*
and *Borderlands*. Other books have expressed a glimpse of the
beyond in our midst: there is *Glimpses of Glory* and *Traces of Glory*.

For much of my life I have lived on the borders of two coun-
tries. I realized that borders are not part of the landscape as much
as what is created by man's mind. At other times I have lived
what has been called 'marginal land'. Marginal land is what some
see as the end of what is comfortable but others have stretched out
beyond and created a good place to live in. To describe the land as
marginal is more about our own vision than the potential of the
land. To stand on the edge and look beyond is to rejoice that life is
greater than we imagined and is only limited by our vision.

My mother used to say I always wanted to see 'the back of
beyond'. This was not just to look around the next bend in the
road but to look deeper into the life I have, and to discover the
mystery of the world about me. A long time ago I scribbled these
headings in a note book:

Everything has a potential to create wonder and awe.
Everything can be a stepping stone into the great unknown.
Every moment is in eternity.
We are explorers of a world with no frontiers.
We are in God and God is in us.
Enjoy!

Against these words I later added a sentence from de Chardin:

'Happy is the man who fails to stifle his vision'.
(Pierre Teilhard de Chardin, *Hymn of the Universe*,
Collins Fontana, 1974, p. 79)

Sadly many have become blind to the greater world that is about us. I do believe it is important to have an informed and scientific outlook, but if that is all we have we have become spiritually impoverished, for it is only part of reality. We need to be able to see not only with the eyes of science but with the eyes of our hearts. Here are some wonderful words from the Letter to the Ephesians:

'I pray also that the eyes of your heart may be enlightened in order that you may know the hope to which he has called you, the riches of his glorious inheritance in the saints, and his incomparably great power for us who believe'. (Ephesians 1.18, 19)

To be without this vision of the world and ourselves is to live without being in touch with the reality of the wonder and mystery that is all about us. It is to live a life without depth. Peter Berger in his book, *A Rumour of Angels*, suggests that the recovery of our senses and our faith will come through the re-opening of our eyes:

A rediscovery of the supernatural will be, above all, a regaining of openness in our perception of reality. It will not only be, as theologians influenced by existentialism have greatly overemphasized, an overcoming of tragedy. Perhaps more importantly it will be an overcoming of triviality. In openness to the signals of the transcendence the true proportions of our experience are rediscovered. This is the comic relief of redemption; it makes it possible for us to laugh and play with a new fullness.
(Peter Berger, *A Rumour of Angels*, Penguin, 1970, p. 119)

Often the eyes of our heart have not been allowed to see deeply or further than is convenient: perhaps we are afraid of being disturbed or disturbing others. If we continue in this shallow view of life we cannot hope to see beyond our narrow vision. There are many worlds about us, and many ways of looking at the world, but we often elect for the narrow view. We allow the clouds to come down and shorten our vision. In choosing one worldview, the other wonders and expansiveness of our own being decrease. Reality becomes for us what seems small and often dull and boring. We get caught up in being too serious or dealing in trivialities all the time. We need to expand again our sense of awe and wonder to look again upon the world with newness and openness. Then like the Celt of old we will see, 'wonder upon wonder and every one of them true'.

If we are so blind to the wonders of the world, how can we hope to behold the mystery and wonder of our God? It is by plunging into the depths and mystery of creation, that we are able to discover the greater wonder of the Creator. It is through the world that God speaks to us, and it is through the created order that we gain our experience and our vision of God. We come to God through creation and our God comes to us through his created order. God and the world are not totally distinct from each other, though God is not dependent on the world, he is to be found within it and we are to discover it is in him. Think upon these wise words:

> God who made man that he might seek him – God whom we try to apprehend by the groping of our lives – that self-same God is as pervasive and perceptible as the atmosphere in which we are bathed. He encompasses us on all sides, like the world itself. What prevents you then, from enfolding him in your arms? Only one thing: your inability to see him . . . The true God, the Christian God, will under your gaze, invade the universe . . . He will penetrate it as a ray of light does a crystal . . . God truly waits for us in things, unless indeed he advances to meet us.
>
> (Pierre Teilhard de Chardin, *Le Milieu Divin*, Collins Fontana, 1975, pp. 46–7)

THE REPOSE OF SLEEP

O God of life, darken not to me Thy light,
O God of life, close not to me Thy joy,
O God of life, shut not to me Thy door,
O God of life, refuse not to me Thy mercy,
O God of life, quench Thou to me Thy wrath,
And O God of life, crown Thou to me Thy gladness,
O God of life, crown Thou to me Thy gladness.

(*Carmina Gadelica* III, p. 343)

This prayer was said once the door was barred for the night and the lamp put out. The house was now in total darkness. But the door to God was still open and the light of God was still in the life of the one who prayed. Even in the darkness God is there. Sleep is a strange thing and even now not greatly understood. There is a feeling that in sleep we enter another world. Yet wherever we are God is there. With God there are no boundaries.

There are many times when we need to seek the door between 'two worlds' to discover they are not two but one. The division is only in our own mind. We are the ones who have created the fences and barriers. Where God dwells is not in a distant world. God is here, God is with us, and above all God is. The division between this world and the kingdom of God is wafer thin, if it exists at all. If there is a threshold to cross, it is as much to do with our mind and heart as with the place we are in. If we are willing to take that step towards God and his kingdom we discover God comes to meet us and that his kingdom comes on earth as we seek to do his will.

Places where we are able to cross a threshold and enter this newness of life are sometimes called liminal places, from the Latin *limen*, meaning a threshold. We cross such a threshold when we begin to seek to live our life; in awareness of the presence and the love of God. Often it is necessary for us to find one such holy place, one open door to God, before we can begin to see that all is holy. It is good to discover your own Holy Island, your own place of the abiding presence and love of God. Even then sometimes we need to find a new threshold to cross, another holy place, until all becomes holy. Know that God keeps such doors open for us.

Such a threshold place, an open door, is shown in the life of Columbanus. Columbanus was born in Leinster about the year 543. As a young man he was advised by a saintly anchoress to take up the religious life. Columbanus was a fine young man and the anchoress could see the local girls had a keen interest in him. There was a danger he might be diverted from his calling. When Columbanus told his mother he intended to join a monastery she was greatly dismayed. She tried to dissuade him. But Columbanus saw the life ahead as one of heroism, adventure and in service of God. On the very day he left home his mother lay across the threshold of the door to prevent him leaving. It is said that Columbanus stepped over his mother and did not look back as he made his way to the community of St Comgall at Bangor. It was a real crossing of a threshold and a turning point in the life of this man of prayer. Other thresholds would come when in mid-life he would leave Bangor for France to build monasteries at Annegray and at Luxeuil, and again when he was 69, as he crossed the Alps into Italy and founded a monastery at Bobbio. Columbanus crossed so many thresholds in the service of God that he described life as 'a road'. We are always called to move forward in our awareness and our love of God.

For me, I knew the day I walked through the door to Kelham Chapel near Newark that I had come to a threshold place. The building, with its great central dome and dark space beneath it, with its great bridge of the sanctuary arch of golden brown bricks upon which stood Sargent Jagger's green, bronzed crucified Christ, was a revelation. Here was a place where men offered themselves to God, where men sought to do the will of God. Brother George Every of the Society of the Sacred Mission said of it in his poem, 'The Rood at Kelham':

> This is a place for human sacrifice
> And on that altar stone young men must die.
> (Reproduced by permission of the Society of the
> Sacred Mission, Willen, Milton Keynes)

For me the building, the singing in plainsong by a strong body of dedicated men, was totally mind-blowing. Here I would learn to die to the selfish self and rise renewed in the service of God. It was here I learnt that it is a thin border of the imagination that separated heaven from earth, or God from us humans. Here I would discover that God is not concerned only with worship or souls but with the whole of life and with all of his creation. At every moment God keeps before us an open door. There are always opportunities to know him, delight in him and serve him. This is not a God confined to Church and worship but one who is to be met in the whole of his creation. I rejoice to read these words by one of the Kelham Fathers:

> Christianity is not concerned with just one aspect or department of human life, but the whole of it. The Church is, or ought to be, concerned not only with how men pray, but with how men make boots, with how men fight, with how men make laws, fall in love, play football, and write sonnets.
>
> (Father Stephen Bedale SSM, speaking at the Kelham reunion, quoted in the SSM Christmas quarterly in 1922)

For me this way of looking at our faith helped to ground it and yet at the same time open all of life up to the eternal. God sets an open door before us all, a door into his presence. Think on the words he said to the church in Philadelphia and act upon them:

> Look, I have set before you an open door, which no one is able to shut.   (Revelation 3.8)

LET THE KING IN

'The King is knocking. If you would have your share of heaven on earth, lift the latch and let the King in' (a woman from Eriskay).

Celtic hospitality was like that of many rural people, they kept an open door. In fact in many places doors were never locked. Hospitality was to be expected of them; though often poor, they would share what they had with a passing stranger. They were afraid that in shutting anyone out they might exclude the Christ. As Christians, they took to heart the saying of Jesus, 'I was a stranger and you welcomed me' (Matthew 25.35). Many were reminded of this by the words of the Celtic Rune of Hospitality:

> I saw a stranger at yestere'en
> I put food in the eating place,
> drink in the drinking place,
> music in the listening place,
> and in the sacred name of the Triune
> He blessed my self and my house,
> my cattle and my dear ones,
> and the lark said in her song,
> often, often, often,
> goes the Christ in stranger's guise.

For the Celt the world of the risen Lord and the 'other world' were never far away. God waits upon us to turn to him and to discover that he is with us. When the woman of Kerry was asked, 'Where is heaven?', she thought long and then said, 'Heaven is about one foot six inches above us'. There is a sense in which we just need to stretch ourselves to begin to enter the kingdom! These people took Jesus at his word when he said, 'The kingdom of heaven is at hand'. God's kingdom is not a 'happy land far, far away' but is near to each of us and we are able to be part of that kingdom by inviting the King into our lives.

The woman from Eriskay was obviously also aware of the text, 'Behold I stand at the door and knock'. These are amazing words from the King of kings. He still comes in humility. Jesus will not force his way in. We can still turn him away. We can still put up a sign that says 'no room'. He will not make us believe or do what he wants us to do. He comes to us in love and can only enter by a return of that love. He will enter by invitation only. Jesus stands on the threshold of our life waiting to share in all that we do. But we have to open the door of our heart to him.

In William Holman Hunt's painting, *The Light of the World*, Jesus is portrayed as standing outside a door. It would appear this door has not been opened for a long time, for briars are growing up around it. Another peculiarity is that the door has no handle. It can only be opened from the inside. Only you can open the door of your heart. God has given you this freedom of choice: you can welcome him into your life or keep him out. You need to learn to say with the early Church, '*Maranatha*, come Lord Jesus'. Jesus awaits your invitation, your welcome. It is no use reading about Jesus or talking about Jesus if we do not rejoice in his presence. I forever worry about groups that meet to talk about Jesus but ignore his presence and do not talk to him. How can you truly study Jesus if you do not know him as the risen Lord and with you? Remember faith is not about doctrine but about your personal relationship with him. One of the worst things that can be said by our Lord to any of us is, 'Truly, I tell you, I do not know you' (Matthew 25.12). Take some time out each day and enjoy the company of our Lord; get to know him. Stop and do it now.

There is much talk of 'thin places' such as Iona or Lindisfarne, and I do believe that some places have a special place in prayer and in the hearts of believers, but every place can be a meeting place with our God. God's presence is not reserved for churches or certain places, though these can vibrate with his presence. Any place, any time, any thing can be a means of meeting with, working with, co-operating with our God. All places are liminal places where God seeks to meet you. Where you are at this moment you can open your heart to God. Now, at this moment, God offers his kingdom to you. It is a gift you can make your own or you can leave it unwrapped, untouched. Learn to tune your senses and open the gift. Then whatever you are doing, whatever your situation you can rejoice in the closeness, and the love of God. To share in his glory is not to be called away from the world but to see the world transformed by seeing it as the instrument of his glory. How I love singing from the Liturgy of St James: 'From glory to glory advancing, we praise thee, O Lord: Thy name with the Father and Spirit be ever adored . . . Evermore, O Lord to thy servants thy presence be nigh.' Know God is waiting at this very moment to reveal his presence to you. Lift the latch and let the King in.

Pray with Christina Rossetti (1830–94):

> Open wide the windows of our spirits and fill us with light:
> open wide the door of our hearts
> that we may receive and entertain Thee with all our powers
>   of adoration.

PETITION

> Be Thou a smooth way before me,
> Be Thou a guiding star above me,
> Be Thou a keen eye behind me,
> This day, this night, for ever.
>
> I am weary and forlorn,
> Lead Thou me to the land of the angels;
> Methinks it were time I went for a space
> To the court of Christ, to the peace of heaven.
>
> If only Thou, O God of life,
> Be at peace with me, be my support,
> Be with me as a star, be to me as a helm
> From my lying down in peace to my rising anew.
>   (*Carmina Gadelica* III, p. 171)

This is a journeying prayer and it fits our journey through life. It is a prayer for guidance and protection throughout the day. There is recognition that even when we travel in the presence of God, as humans we still become tired and need rest. The desire to be with Christ in the land of angels for a while is not to escape the world but to seek refreshment and renewal and so be enabled to continue our journey without getting lost or overcome. It is a great art to step out of our busyness or our weariness and to enter into the peace of God. Those who say they are too busy for prayer are too busy! It is a matter of priorities, and if God is not among our priorities we have got it wrong. In fact you cannot truly believe in God if you do not turn to him regularly. In the very midst of your busyness learn to take time out. There is need to take the words of Jesus seriously when he says, 'Come to me, all you that are weary and carrying heavy burdens, and I will give you rest' (Matthew 11.28). In a balanced life there must be time for rest, for quiet and for enjoying the presence of God. There is a lovely story of Antony of Egypt and the need for rest:

> Once Abbot Antony was talking with some of his brethren and a game-hunter came where they were. He saw the brothers enjoying themselves and expressed his disapproval. Antony said: 'Put an arrow in the bow and shoot it.' He did this and Antony said 'now shoot another, and another'. This continued for a good while and the hunter said: 'If I bend my bow all the time it will break.' Antony replied, 'So it is with the work of God. If we push ourselves beyond measure the brethren will soon collapse. It is right from time to time to relax.'

We need to learn to unbend and trust in God rather than forever in our own efforts.

In these days of so many stressed people, it is important to show the peace of God in our lives. Learn to live in the presence, in the peace and in the power of God. Affirm that God is with you. You are not alone. Rejoice in this reality throughout the day. Remind yourself, the Lord his here, his Spirit is with us. This does not distract us from our work; in fact it will strengthen us in what we do. You can use this affirmation many times on your journey to work and when you are busy. You can go for a space to the court of Christ and the peace of heaven. The busier life becomes, and the more burdened it is, the more you need to be able to do this. Know that in his presence is peace. Often in the very middle of a storm, or at the height of busyness, I say:

> Lord grant me your peace,
> Peace in my heart and in my dealings,
> Peace in my life and my relationships,
> Peace in this day and all that comes to me,
> The deep peace of God which passes all understanding.

It is good to know that the peace we seek is a gift from God. It is not of our own making. We can rest in his peace as someone enjoys the warmth of the sun. There is no need for effort on our part, only to place ourselves where we can receive it. It is no use asking for peace and at the same time rushing about like mad. Take moments to let the peace of God enter your life. It is a wonderful way to begin the day. Far too many of us set off at a rush. Start the day in stillness basking in the presence of God allowing his peace into your day. Five minutes spent in this way in the morning can transform your whole day. It is worth setting aside the time to open your life to the reality that God is with you on your journey this day.

> Be still and know God is with you.
> He comes with all his gifts.
> He offers his peace and his love to you.
> Relax in his presence.
> Let the love of God fill you and your home.
> Let the deep, deep peace of God enfold you.
> Let his peace enter your life and your heart.
> You may like to ask for his guidance in what you are to do,
>   or for his protection.
> Seek his blessing upon your home and your work.
>
> And the peace of God, which surpasses all understanding,
>   will guard your hearts and minds in Christ Jesus.
>   (Philippians 4.7)

THE PATH OF LIGHT

> Though the dawn breaks cheerless on this Isle today,
> My spirit walks upon a path of light.
> For I know my greatness,
> Thou hast built me a throne within Thy heart.
> I dwell safely within the circle of Thy care.
> I cannot for a moment fall out of the everlasting arms.
> I am on my way to glory.
>   (Alistair Maclean, *Hebridean Altars*,
>   Hodder & Stoughton, 1999, p. 25)

This prayer honestly faces the reality of the 'cheerless isle'. All days are not made up of sunshine, some days are absolutely awful and have very little to commend them. As believers we do not escape from the trials and tribulations of humankind. I used this prayer on Holy Island on many a cold damp winter's morning in church. I used it when the island was storm-tossed and the sea was raging. There is no use denying the reality of what is around you. There is need to face the truth of the situation you are in, but make sure it is the whole truth and not just what is making demands at the moment.

I also saw that 'this isle' was myself, that I had cheerless and dark days. Like all humans, sometimes life feels awful! But feelings are only half the picture; they are like looking at a negative of flowers and thinking, that is the way they look. We need to get the whole picture in view for there is far more to this world than we see or feel. Even when dreadful things are happening and all may seem lost, we need to keep a vision of whom we belong to and what is our long-term future. We need to assure ourselves of the presence and the power of our God.

I say this prayer on cheerless days because of the lines that follow, and so tune in to a greater reality. This is not just positive thinking, it is to help make oneself aware of the presence and the love of God. Even in the darkest day know this love is also a reality. Such faith has sustained many a saint and many a believer in times of trouble.

Days can be cheerless: everything may appear to be against you. But an awareness of the love and protection of God can change everything. You can see the light – at least at the end of the tunnel – and you can turn towards it. Learn to walk in a path of light; know that nothing can separate you from the love of God in Christ Jesus. When I lived on the North Yorkshire Moors the valleys often filled with cloud and all was grey and dull, but if I travelled a short distance I could walk or drive in brilliant sunshine along the moorland ridges. Looking down on the cloud from there it was no longer grey but fluffy white and quite beautiful. In the dark days we need to learn to shift our perspective and see we are not alone and that the darkness is not total; it is only a small

116

part of our reality. The Celts weathered many a storm by knowing that God loves them, and so they turned to walk in a path of light.

Discover your own greatness! You come from God, belong to God, will return to God: even now, you are in the heart of God. Say with St Paul, 'Nothing can separate me from the love of God in Christ Jesus'. How wonderful you are, to be loved by God! Or rather how wonderful is the love of God to go out to you and me. Know that God values you and your life and he will not let you perish.

Wherever you go, whatever you do, whatever is done to you, God loves you and will never leave. You are under his care. No matter where you stray or where life takes you, he is always there. You cannot fall for a moment out of the everlasting arms. I like to think that the hands that uphold us bear the nail marks from the cross. Our Saviour has shared in all our sufferings and is ever ready to help us. In his love he seeks to enfold us, to embrace us. We do not know what lies ahead but we know who goes with us and is there to meet us.

Our journey has an end, here described as 'glory'. Our journey is from the temporal to the eternal, from that which is passing and perishable to that which is imperishable and lasting. We will not be absorbed by the glory of God, for we will keep our personality, that which is essentially us. We will not be lost in God but rather we will find the fullness of life in him and in his love. Rejoice in the fact that you are a child of God, you are loved by him, known by your own name and you are on your way to glory. I end with one of my favourite prayers from St Augustine of Hippo. I use this prayer at funerals and any time when the cheerless day descends:

> All shall be Amen and Alleluia.
> We shall rest and we shall see,
> We shall see and we shall know,
> We shall know and we shall love,
> We shall love and we shall praise.
> Behold our end which is no end.